What A Writer Needs

Ralph Fletcher

With a Foreword by
Donald M. Murray

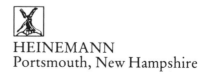

HEINEMANN
Portsmouth, New Hampshire

Heinemann

361 Hanover Street, Portsmouth, NH 03801-3912
Offices and agents throughout the world

The author and publisher are grateful to the following for granting permission to reprint
copyrighted material:

Page 5: "Mother Nature" by Gary Snyder. Reprinted by permission of New Directions
Paperback.

Page 5: Excerpt from *Amos and Boris* by William Steig. Copyright © 1971 by William
Steig. Reprinted by permission of Farrar, Straus & Giroux.

Page 51: From *The Two of Them* by Aliki. Copyright © 1979 by Aliki Brandenberg. By
permission of Greenwillow Books, a division of William Morrow & Company, Inc.

Page 59: From *Miss Maggie* by Cynthia Rylant. Copyright © 1983 by Cynthia Rylant. Used
by permission of Dutton Children's Books, a division of Penguin Books, USA, Inc.

Page 84: Excerpt from *Tuck Everlasting* by Natalie Babbitt. Copyright © 1975 by Natalie
Babbitt. Reprinted by permission of Farrar, Straus & Giroux.

Page 94: "Poem" from *The Dream Keeper and Other Poems* by Langston Hughes.
Copyright © 1932 by Alfred A. Knopf, Inc. and renewed 1960 by Langston Hughes.
Reprinted by permission of the publisher.

Pages 96, 99: *A Father Like That* by Charlotte Zolotow. Text copyright © 1971 by
Charlotte Zolotow. Selection reprinted by permission of HarperCollins Publishers.

Page 111: "Watermelons" from *Return to a Place Lit By a Glass of Milk* by Charles Simic.
Copyright © 1974 by Charles Simic. Reprinted by permission of George Braziller, Inc.

Page 118: *Julie of the Wolves* by Jean Craighead George. Text copyright © 1972 by Jean
Craighead George. Selection reprinted by permission of HarperCollins Publishers.

Every effort has been made to contact copyright holders for permission to reprint
borrowed material where necessary, but if any oversights have occurred, we would be
happy to rectify them in future printings of this work.

Library of Congress Cataloging-in-Publication Data
Fletcher, Ralph J.
    What a writer needs / Ralph Fletcher.
      p.   cm.
    Includes bibliographical references (p.) and index.
    ISBN 0-435-08734-7
    1. English language—Composition and exercises—Study and teaching
(Elementary)—United States. 2. English language—Composition and
exercises—Study and teaching (Secondary)—United States.
  I. Title
LB1576.F483 1992
372.6′23–dc20   92-24344
                                  CIP

Printed on acid-free paper.
Designed by Joni Doherty.
Printed in the United States of America.

12 11 10 RRD 30 29 28 27 26 25 24

FOR MY FATHER
Ralph Joseph Fletcher

Contents

Foreword

DONALD M. MURRAY

UNIQUE. *What a Writer Needs* by Ralph Fletcher is *unique*. George Minot, my first apoplectic editor, exploded when I used the word *unique* in a news story. I can still hear his bellow echoing back and forth across the City Room: "Murray, nothing is unique in the world." Well, Ralph Fletcher's new book is unique.

I have read—and bought—most of the books on writing published since I was in high school half a century ago and most of the books on teaching writing since 1963, and I have not read another book that does what this one does.

Fletcher serves many readers, a professional challenge in itself. *What a Writer Needs* will be a valuable text and resource book for the teacher who wants to write; it will be just as valuable for the teacher who does not want to write but wants to teach writing; it will also be valuable for students in kindergarten through twelfth grade as its lessons are passed down through teachers and in many cases learned directly from Fletcher as teachers read from the book or pass it to individual students.

What struck me first about the manuscript is that it is written by a serious, well-trained writer who is dedicated to his craft. Most books on writing for teachers are written by teachers, researchers, theorists, experts on something they do not do. Many have important and insightful things to say, but as a writer, when I read these books by nonwriters, I often feel as if I were reading a traveler's account written by someone who had visited my country for six weeks or less and then gone home to write. Fletcher is a writer who writes of writing as a writer, and teachers need to hear someone who writes with wisdom, intimacy, love, and joy of our daily discipline.

The book is an autobiography. Reading this book you will observe a writer's education as Fletcher reports on what and how his teachers taught him and allows the reader to share his continual apprenticeship to our craft. His story is—as good writing always is—intensely personal and universal. I learn from his private story and, at the same time, know it is my story.

What a Writer Needs breaks down the writer's craft and teaches what the writer has to learn and relearn at the writing desk. Fletcher speaks of writing from the maker's side of the workbench in language that is lively and easy to understand. It is a profound but accessible book.

Fletcher also speaks as one who is at home in the classroom. He is a master teacher who combines delight and affection for children with a teacher's discipline. He builds sturdy bridges from the writer's studio to the elementary and middle school classroom. *What a Writer Needs* would be worth reading as a textbook on teaching.

I am also surprised at how successful—how unique—*What a Writer Needs* is as a book on reading. First a confession. I find most student papers reprinted in academic articles and books remarkably uninteresting, boring, unbelievable. They may have been wonderful in the context of a class but they do not travel well. The magic is gone. This is *not* true of Fletcher's book. He uses examples of young students' writing in every chapter that impress and instruct me. These young writers are believable, and they each demonstrate an important lesson in craft.

But Fletcher goes beyond that. His book is the only book I know that connects the writing of young students with publishing writers. He combines young people's writing with his own adult writing and with many examples of published writers. His book is a textbook in reading, showing how a writer reads and how that way of reading can enrich the experience of students studying writing *and* reading, two language arts that should be connected but, despite all the rhetoric, rarely are.

And as a writer who is often amused and angered by dreadful writing in books advocating good writing, I find Fletcher's book graceful, lively, and in a wonderful way unassuming. He is never the pompous authority. He never speaks down; he is, rather, the writer/teacher at work, looking up with surprise and delight as you open the door of his study. He invites you in by saying, "Come in, I'm having fun."

Accept his invitation. You will have fun, very wise fun.

Acknowledgments

"Thou canst not stir a flower without troubling of a star," Francis Thompson once wrote. I like that. It reminds me that we are connected in unfathomable ways, and it gives me pause as I try to acknowledge the roots, both early and immediate, of this book.

Many people made helpful suggestions for the Appendix: Betty Blankfein, Fredda Klopfer and the Bagels & Pens group at the Glen Head Elementary School, JoAnn Curtis, Martha Horn, Suzanne Gardiner. I am particularly indebted to Linda Rief, Carol Wilcox, and Lisa Lenz for all their help.

Suggestions by Brenda Power and Dawne Boyer, my editor, were enormously helpful in the text itself. More than anyone else, Dawne helped me shape this text into its final form.

Thanks to my wife JoAnn. She has heard much of it from me before but always manages to find a set of fresh new eyes to read my stuff. She has had a profound impact on all my thinking about teaching writing, and on many passages in this book.

Thanks to all the students whose writing appears in this book.

As for deeper roots:

The "Mentors" chapter allows me to reflect on those teachers who profoundly influenced my writing. But certain people are not mentioned in that chapter. I am grateful to the many literate writing teachers I have had over the years—Denis Thompson at West Islip High School, Jon Appleton and Jim Heffernan at Dartmouth, Charles McGrath and Gail Godwin at Columbia. By taking my writing seriously, these people made it possible for me to take myself seriously as a writer.

Thanks to my kids. Every day Taylor, Adam, and Robert amaze (exhaust) me by how hard they play. I have learned from them so many things, not to take myself too seriously and, lately, that writing itself is a kind of sustained play, playing hard with language.

At the Teachers College Writing Project, I sometimes felt funny about talking like a writer to New York City teachers. I feared I would be erecting a wall between myself and the teacher I was working with. Lucy Calkins helped me to see that bringing my expertise as a writer into the classroom was a way of finding my own voice as a teacher.

ACKNOWLEDGMENTS

Many of these ideas were at least partially sculpted by the intense dialogues I had with other colleagues at the Writing Project: Lucy Calkins, JoAnn Curtis, Jenifer Hall, Shelley Harwayne, Georgia Heard, Martha Horn, Karen Howell, Jim Sullivan. I have left that community now, but those discussions have a way of reverberating in my head whenever I'm thinking about writing.

Thanks to Bill Martin Jr. I once watched Bill working with a group of young writers and was astonished at the incredible respect with which he listened to and commented on their work. I hope a tiny bit of that has trickled down into my own work with children.

I have been fortunate to receive encouragement from many people in my family, especially my mother and my uncles Paul Fletcher and John Fletcher. Thanks also to Cliff Proctor, Mark Mittelman, Arthur Voigt, Roland Barth, Nancie Atwell, Tom Newkirk, Lisa Siemens, Jim Vojcsik, and Rob Cohen.

Thanks to my brothers and sisters who have kept my spirits up during tough times.

Thanks to Don Murray. My first encounter reading Murray's books on writing left me dazzled—it forever altered both my teaching and my writing. I have a fair imagination but I never dreamed that one day he might write the foreword to a book of mine. It is a great honor to have his name on this book.

One of the surprises in creating this book was all the writing about my father that kept surfacing. If I imagine my writing as a river, I know that much of its source water lies in my family, in my father. I have learned a great deal from my dad—I'm proud to share his name.

Introduction

IT HAPPENED in a classroom one frigid November morning when the clouds were hanging low and steely in the sky. At precisely 11:03 the third-grade teacher glimpsed something, a fraying hint of whiteness outside the classroom window.

"It's starting to snow!" she said to her class. The kids looked up. Blinked. "Come here. Over to the window. We'll open the blinds up and take a good look at it."

The children hurried over, eager to eyeball the year's first snowfall. Innumerable fat flakes parachuting down. One boy held back and stayed at his desk.

"Come on, Brent," the teacher urged. "Join us."

But Brent was adamant.

"Don't do it!" he cried to the other kids. "Don't look! She'll make us write!"

I love this story because it reminds me not to get too evangelical about teaching writing. Teaching writing is hard work. As writing teachers, we come upon every imaginable kind of thorny problem: students who hate to write, who lack confidence and write poorly, who love to write but can't read back what they have written, who can't spell, can't conjugate, can't punctuate . . .

Most children do learn to write, more or less. But how do we, as teachers and/or parents, sustain and extend this natural development? Much of their growth will come through independent work: writing a great deal, reading widely and deeply, discovering useful writing strategies borrowed from professional writers.

But there is no way around it: Our students will also learn to write from us.

Writing teachers draw upon three distinct areas of expertise. We must know our students. We must know how to teach. And we must know something about writing itself. Many fine texts on teaching writing have explored child-watching and methodology. This book concerns itself with the art and craft of writing itself. I hope the reader of this book will get a better grasp on how writing works, both in its parts and as a whole.

Odysseus learned to steer his ship between Scylla and Charybdis, mythological monsters who bedeviled and devoured all sailors who dared attempt that narrow passage. In this book I imagine myself trying a similarly tricky navigation. On one side the book risks running aground on the rocks of dense theory. Writing is a complicated business that can get you neck-deep into a scholarly rumination on linguistics, etymology, or semiotics if you're not careful. A writer might even select a single element of writing, such as *voice* or *character,* and expand it into an entire book.

At the other side, I knew for certain I did not want to write a writing recipe book: one fresh lead, two teaspoons sequence, a pinch of voice, etc. Writing just doesn't work that way.

I have tried to find the middle ground: a practical book about writing. I have included strategies that a writer might use immediately in his or her own writing. Not all writers make good writing teachers (and vice versa). While apprenticing as a writer, and gathering an impressive portfolio of rejection slips, I cherished the advice from writers I respected who were willing to share their secrets with me, who could help me find a way through the complexities of this dizzying craft to what Donald Murray calls the "unifying simplicities" underneath.

This is no recipe book: I have tried not to be formulaic. Rather, I want to suggest the richness of options, the myriad possibilities open to the writer at any given moment. Young writers need to know what can be done with language. The strategies and suggestions included here might be thought of as the colors on an artist's palette. The artist begins by learning color, primary and secondary, highlight and shade. This is only the beginning. Ultimately, it's up to the artist to decide when and if to use a particular color in a painting.

Any writing text must include concrete examples. I have drawn them from several sources—my own writing, the writing of students and teachers, and literature: fiction, poetry, articles, picture books. These examples were not selected for grade-level applicability; some are probably not appropriate for children at all. Don Graves is right: Writing/reading teachers must begin with our own literacy. Even with very young children, we need to bring a wealth of knowledge to our understanding of their writing. The examples in this book were selected to broaden and deepen that knowledge.

The inclusion of picture books may raise a few eyebrows among teachers who work with older students, but picture books (see Appendix) can be terrific tools for exploring writing with students of all ages. A picture book like *Owl Moon* by Jane Yolen is subtle, beautifully written, eminently rereadable. The best books of this genre have a lovely transparency that make them perfect for talking about writing. They contain all the classical literary elements (leads, conflict, protagonist, resolution, etc.) without the numbing volume of details, incidents, and characters that make it nearly impossible for students to grasp such elements by themselves.

Writing this book, and answering for myself the questions it raised, helped distill my own ideas about writing. What are the fundamental elements of good writing? Is it possible to prioritize (hate that word) them? Is voice more important than character? Should I include specific writing exercises for the young writer to practice?

The question of writing exercises unearths memories of my first overnight camping trip with the Boy Scouts. After all the tents had been set up, the oldest boys in our troop gathered the youngest boys together. Eight of us, Tenderfeet all, gazed up expectantly at the bigger boys.

"We've got a problem—we're missing some important stuff," one of the oldest boys said in a low and serious voice. "We're going to have a tough time without it, too."

"Yeah," another boy said. "We forgot to bring the bacon-stretcher. Can't cook bacon over a campfire without it."

"That's not all," another boy said glumly. "There's the sky hook. Kenny, I can't believe you left that home."

"Bad news," the first boy said. "We're going to need that stuff. Look, I'm going to split you kids up. You four go over to that camp and ask the Scout Master if we can borrow their bacon-stretcher. You four go the other way, to that campsite just over that ridge. See if they'll let us use their sky hook. At least til tomorrow. See if they have an extra one."

I felt proud to be trusted to take part in such an important mission. I went with the kids in search of the bacon-stretcher. The Scout Master of the troop camped directly next to us listened carefully to our request, rubbed his forehead, shook his head solemnly, and sent us to another camp. From there we were sent to another camp. It took nearly two hours of trudging around before someone mercifully let us in on the joke.

True, not all writing exercises are as maliciously useless as sky hooks and bacon-stretchers. But many are. I watched a teacher read *The Lorax* by Dr. Seuss to her students. These were big kids, eighth graders, and they were riveted. She had them.

"Now, I want you to write a letter to Mr. Onesler," she told the students. "Tell him how you feel about the way he's been chopping down all the trees."

That broke the spell. The kids sighed, slumped. They knew only too well Mr. Onesler was a fictitious character. No one would read the letters. The exercise lacked any authentic purpose.

I know several writers who found certain writing exercises helpful in college or graduate writing programs, and I do include a few in this book. But I think we need to be wary of them, particularly for elementary or junior high writers. Here's my belief: You don't learn to write by going through a series of preset writing exercises. You learn to write by grappling with a real subject that truly matters to you.

In the first part of this book I explore the essential conditions that allowed me to become a writer—finding mentors I could look up to, learning to take risks, building on a love of words—and how these conditions might nourish young writers in a classroom setting. In Part Two, I take a closer look at a dozen tools that writers use nearly every day: balancing the specific with the general, creating character and a sense of place, beginnings and endings, juggling the issue of time, and so forth.

I tried to choose those elements of writing that are not specific to any one genre but could help writers develop their craft in many different kinds of writing. Developing character may be a prime concern of the fiction writer or journalist, but it can also be crucially important to the historian or poet. Journalists do not have a monopoly on the use of research, nor do poets with metaphor.

One danger of having discrete chapters in a book such as this one is that it may suggest a segmented, compartmentalized approach to writing. In fact, no element of writing can exist in isolation. If a poem or essay works at all, it works as an organic unit with every part contributing almost invisibly to the total effect of the piece. Every part, every *word*, depends upon its relationship to the whole. When we talk about the different elements or components of writing, it may be helpful to conceive of them as different lenses, fresh perspectives, through which we can view the gestalt and understand more clearly how the writing works.

I once heard Gary Snyder read the following poem:

Mother Nature

She is not a sheath:
She is a quiver.

Snyder has had a profound effect on my own poetry, so it was with some trepidation that I approached him after the reading and introduced myself. For me, at least, it was a heart-stopping literary moment: The man standing right next to Snyder was none other than Allen Ginsberg. Ginsberg's eyes twinkled while he listened.

"I didn't understand that poem 'Mother Nature,' " I confessed.

"Well, do you know the Latin word for 'sheath?' " Snyder asked me impatiently.

"No, I don't know Latin," I admitted. Snyder looked piteously, first at Ginsberg, then back to me.

"Look, you've got to know Latin. Look it up." He sighed. "A sheath holds but one thing, right? A quiver holds many arrows. Mother Nature holds many things . . ."

I retreated, enlightened if chagrined. And as I prepared to write this book, I lugged around a large accordion file, each slot labelled with the appropriate element of writing: BEGINNINGS, ENDINGS, CHARACTER, TIME, SETTING, DETAILS, etc. Whenever and wherever I found a wonderful ending, I made a copy and filed it accordingly. But many bits of writing did not fit smoothly into one particular category. These pieces of writing, like Mother Nature in Snyder's poem, contained many things and resisted my attempt to boil them down to one essential element. Consider this passage from William Steig's *Amos and Boris*, a terrific picture book about a friendship between a whale (Boris) and a mouse (Amos):

> Swimming along, sometimes at great speed, sometimes slowly and leisurely, sometimes resting and exchanging ideas, sometimes stopping to sleep, it took them a week to reach Amos's home shore. During that time they developed a deep admiration for one another. Boris admired the delicacy, the quivering daintiness, the light touch, the small voice, the gemlike radiance of the mouse. Amos admired the bulk, the grandeur, the power, the purpose, the rich voice, and the abounding friendliness of the whale.

Where in my accordion file did this passage belong? Compare and contrast? Characterization? Tension? Sparkling language? Words? Humor? Voice? This passage is a quiver—no matter how hard I try, it refuses to be a sheath.

It is inevitable that teachers use labels or pet names when talking about writing. My colleague Karen Howell asks children to reread and look for the *hot spot* in their stories. This phrase gives the novice writer a new way to reread a narrative. I have suggested that students might conceive of a story as a river going over a waterfall.

"Be careful you don't start your story too far upstream," I cautioned one group of fifth graders. "When I write, I usually want the reader to be able to hear the faint roar from that waterfall right at the beginning."

Metaphors like these can help students internalize complex writing issues by rooting the issue in a concrete, sensuous image.

However, labels can also be dangerous. They risk cheapening the prose or poem by diminishing our thinking about it rather than opening it up. A story, after all, is not a river coursing over a waterfall. In most ways, narratives and rivers obey laws quite distinct from one another. Writing teachers need to be careful when using verbal shorthand to talk about complicated subjects. We need to think hard about how we talk about writing—to our colleagues, to our students, to ourselves. Language, as the linguists tell us, is also the language of thought. In the end, the words we use to explain such concepts to our students will be the words they use to explain them to themselves.

PART ONE
Essentials

ONE
Mentors

I have come to the frightening conclusion that I am the decisive element in the classroom. It's my personal approach that creates the climate. It's my daily mood that makes the weather. As a teacher, I possess tremendous power to make a child's life miserable or joyous. I can be a tool of torture or an instrument of inspiration. I can humiliate or humor, hurt or heal.
HAIM GINOTT

DURING my college senior year I took a creative writing seminar with the novelist Caulder Willingham. Willingham had written ten novels as well as screenplays for *Little Big Man* and *The Graduate*.

Caulder Willingham. The very name sounded literary. He was a Southerner, a tall, red-haired man with gangly limbs and a bourbon nose. We met at an off-campus apartment the college rented for him every Wednesday night. There were ten students in the class. He always had on hand plenty of rolls, cold cuts, chips, pickles, beer, wine, and Teachers Scotch. Class went from 7 to 9 P.M. But we rarely left before 11, and many of us left a bit unsteadily at that.

Willingham dissected our stories, three per night. We loved this man; we soaked up every facial expression he made in response to our work, his most casual aside. He had emphatic tastes about literature—prejudices, he would be the first to admit—and did not shy away from sharing them with us. It didn't take much to touch off some of Willingham's diatribes.

"Tell me a *story*," he'd thunder. "I don't care how smart you are, how philosophical you get. If you don't tell me a story I'm not going to want to read more than a few pages. And beware 'purple prose'—the disease of modern writing, if you ask me. When you write you should be asking yourself: *What* am I trying to say? And say it."

On the night of our last class, Willingham sat before us in a tweed jacket and black tie. He held a stack of long white envelopes in his hand.

"I didn't teach this class for the money," he said softly. "I decided to teach this class to repay a favor. When I was a young writer, James T. Farrell took me under his wing a little bit and helped me out. He told me, 'Someday, you might be able to help out a struggling writer yourself.' That's why I'm teaching this class. What he said is still true today, maybe truer than ever. There's a lot of young writers out there. Someday you might be able to lend them a hand."

He took out the envelopes and lay them in his lap.

"Here's what I've done. The college has paid me sixteen hundred bucks to teach this course. I've taken that amount and subtracted everything I spent on booze and what-not. That leaves about a thousand dollars, even. What I've done is divide that amount among the members of this class. Nobody is getting less than a B. A B gets you fifty bucks. An A gets you a hundred bucks, and an A with a citation will get you a hundred and fifty bucks."

We gasped, laughed.

"First, Mr. Shnayerson . . ." Willingham said, clearing his throat and smiling to himself as he fingered the first envelope.

I'll never forget Caulder Willingham (though I'm not sure I endorse monetary rewards for the writers in our classrooms). His words are well worth remembering for all of us who work with young writers: "There's a lot of young writers out there. Someday you might be able to lend them a hand."

Our classrooms are filled with students desperate for adults who care about writing and books as much as they do. As teachers, we find ourselves in a unique position to be mentors for these emerging writers. If for whatever reason we cannot do so, we should encourage our students to find someone else—an uncle, a librarian, another teacher—who can fill that crucial role.

When I first envisioned this book, I imagined tucking a chapter on mentors near the back, just before the Appendix, perhaps. It seemed like a fine, if predictable way to finish—young writers need adults who can help them reach new horizons, and so forth. It didn't take long for me to revise my thinking. I was struck by how often I go back to the advice of those adults who shaped me as a young writer. No, the mentor chapter would not suffice as after-dinner mint: It had to be part of the main course. For one thing, such a chapter would allow me to grapple with the ghosts of all those people who most powerfully sculpted my psyche—for better and for worse—as a young writer.

Mrs. Damon was my first-grade teacher. The photograph of our class, where I am firmly wedged between Steve Fishman and Pamela Coyne, reveals Mrs. Damon to be a gray-haired woman, slightly stocky, in a starchy white blouse. All business, this woman. Mrs. Damon was more than the first writing mentor I encountered at school. For me, Mrs. Damon *was* school. Her moods, her high standards, created the emotional landscape through which I moved and thought and labored that first school year.

I revered this woman. It pained me to live with the knowledge that while I excelled in many areas, I consistently let Mrs. Damon down in one: My handwriting was horrific. I simply could not get my fingers to make the pencil dance the way a pencil should dance. My letters leaned, wandered, wobbled, and trembled so violently even I could not read them most of the time. I drooled over the perfectly printed papers the girls in our class produced with such apparent effortlessness. No matter how hard I tried, I could not replicate anything even approaching their work. In that class-room, writing *was* penmanship, and no paper of mine ever received higher than a C.

One day I got a paper back with a D- scrawled on the top. (The minus next to the D seemed to slope down, a grieving elephant with drooped trunk.) I took the paper home, crumpled it up, and hid it under a rock that was painted white in the front corner of our yard. Later, I retrieved the wrinkled paper and shamefully showed it to my parents.

Mrs. Damon took a vigilant stance toward my penmanship problem. She made it *our* problem, and set me to work on rectifying it. My nightly homework assignments included practicing the alphabet by printing all twenty-six letters five times on five separate sheets of paper. Each sheet had to be signed by my mother and handed in promptly the following morning.

One afternoon Mrs. Damon took me aside and looked deeply into my eyes.

"Listen, Ralph," she said softly. "You're going to have to work harder on this. You've got sloppy penmanship, and sloppy penmanship means a sloppy personality."

A sloppy personality! Had the words come from anyone else, I might have been able to shrug them off. From her, I could not. Mrs. Damon, how could you say such a thing to me? It was you who taught me to add and subtract, to recite the Pledge of Allegiance, to sing "America the Beautiful." You taught me to read. I trusted you: I listened. I could as easily ignore your words as my own mother's. Your judgments bore deep holes in my soul. Years later I would learn the ins and outs of motor coordination, large and small. I would learn about developmental lags. I would learn that a writer might indeed have ambitions beyond neat penmanship. But in first grade I was branded with a sloppy personality. And I never quite got over it.

During the years that followed, I endured what passed for writing in school. All the important writing I did took place at home. I started writing little books, a series about a baseball rookie named Carlos who breaks into the majors to tremendous acclaim. Carlos was a phenom: the kid could do no wrong. Veteran pitchers scratched their heads, concocted new pitches like "space balls" and "submarine balls," anything to get Carlos out. This was a natural topic for me because sports books were just about all I was reading: *The Willie Mays Story, My Turn at Bat* by Ted Williams, *It's Good to Be Alive* by Roy Campanella.

By high school I had become a serious reader: Novels were my mentors. Anything by Poe, Hemingway, Fitzgerald, Dostoyevsky, Dickens. *One Flew over the Cuckoo's Nest* by Ken Kesey. *Going After Cacciato* by Tim O'Brien. Tolkien and Frank Norris. Brautigan and D. H. Lawrence. I'd gulp them down with indiscriminate naivete—pop books and classics—before passing them on to my younger brothers and sisters. I watched my brother Jim become so enchanted by Gabriel García Márquez's master-piece, *One Hundred Years of Solitude,* that in an act of near masochistic discipline he rationed himself to twenty-five pages per night to make the book last as long as possible. When the book finally came my way I discovered that I lacked his mettle; I consumed the thick novel in four or five lengthy swallows.

Books like these tore me up inside. What an incredible thing, to be able to affect adults and children, total strangers, people in other countries, with nothing but words, words forged out of your own experience, your own heart, your own imagination!

In graduate school I took several courses with Richard Price. He was just a few years older than myself (mentors don't necessarily have to be old, white-haired, bearded) and had just finished his fourth novel, *The Breaks.* He would later go on to Hollywood to become a successful screenwriter. Price's seminars were dominated by his wit, which could be scathing at times, though he generally delivered his most barbed lines with smiling good humor.

"Your narrator needs an alarm clock," he told one student. "He's sleep-walking through your story. Wake him up!"

"You're telling us on page nine that the mother still misses her kid," Price said another time. "Hey, guess what? We got that on page *two.* Come on. Trust your reader. Where are you going with this?"

Certain writers in the seminar (myself included) tended to get overly didactic in our stories, or sink our sentences with too much heavy-handed philosophizing. One day Price took issue with it.

"You're getting awfully preachy in this story," he told one of my peers. "A lot of writers here have the same problem. If you want to send a message, go to Western Union."

Everyone laughed. The remark hit home.

A mentor relationship between an experienced writer and novice can take many forms. But my own mentors, and the teachers I know who are real mentors to the young writers they work with, have certain things in common.

A MENTOR HAS HIGH STANDARDS

I once spent a week in New Orleans with the late poet Robert Stock, a contemporary of Jack Kerouac and Kenneth Rexroth. Stock was a tall man with long silver hair and a beautiful, ruined face. I would stay up late with him while he managed to drink gin, watch old movies, and read poetry in the original Brazilian, all at the same time. He was very generous to me and encouraged me to show him some poetry I had written.

"I like this poem," I said, "but it's not quite done. There's one word here, in this line, that isn't quite right."

He burst out laughing.

"I must have thrown away a hundred poems for that reason," he said. "Because a single word wasn't right."

Stock's fanatical perfectionism made an indelible impression on me. A mentor does not praise mediocre work. A mentor knows the sound and the feel of language skillfully used. The novice writer, who is becoming alive to the possibilities of language, respects that.

The mentor's high standards inspire the young writer not to lower his or her own standards. In the early 1980s I wrote to a friend, the poet David Fisher, the good news that I had just had an article accepted for publication in *Cosmopolitan* magazine. Fisher was not impressed.

"Forget *Cosmopolitan*," he wrote back to me. "Think Thomas Mann. Think Virginia Woolf."

A MENTOR BUILDS ON STRENGTHS

"Kill your darlings," Richard Price used to say, urging us to discover our own bad writing tendencies and ruthlessly ferret them out. This suggestion was helpful to semi-proficient writers in a graduate seminar. But exhorting very young writers (or students who write without confidence) to kill their darlings may do more harm than good: Once the "darlings" have been killed off in a student's writing there may not be much left that is still alive.

Like a good music teacher, the writing teacher endures the bad melodies and shaky rhythms, stays patient, and picks out moments when the writing works well. It might be but a sentence: "The rollercoaster went upside down and stopped like a bat hanging from a tree." It might be in a single phrase. Even in a "bad" piece of writing, the mentor reaches into the chaos, finds a place where the writing works, pulls it from the wreckage, names it, and makes the writer aware of this emerging skill with words. Careful praise of this kind can fuel a writer for a long time.

Most students write far far better than they will ever know. We have to let children in on the secret of how powerfully they write. We need to let them take inspiration from what they already do well. Consider this disturbing poem by a third-grade boy from Queens, something that might never get published in a conventional press or magazine because of its searing honesty.

> *My Life*
>
> My life is like
> a garbage truck:
> Saturdays and Sundays off.
> Monday
> Tuesday
> Wednesday
> Thursday
> Friday
> they haul you
> away.

The following poem by a second grader in New York City was inspired by Nan Fry's poem, "The Apple":

> *The Corn*
>
> The
>   corn
>   is
>   like
>   a
>   maze
> through all its kernels on the cob.
> In the middle of the holes
> there is darkness
> and over it
> the sunny bright sky.

What a clever pun on the word *maze!* Deliberate? Of course not. But skilled writers learn how to take advantage of the pleasant surprises that crop up in their writing. The teacher pointed it out to her; they looked up the word "maize" in the dictionary. Before long the girl was beaming as if she had planned the pun herself.

I read *The Two of Them* by Aliki to a class of Long Island second graders. The children and I discussed the book and, later, Christine Martinez wrote this tribute to her grandfather:

> My grandpa gave Heather my sister a necklace and when I was born my grandpa gave me a ring and last year it fit me and this year he died. He died on January 5, 1991, the beginning of the year. When I went to his house we played cards and we also played a guessing game. And we planted flowers. And when he died my grandma told me that the flowers died. I was the one who cryed the most. My mom's friend Ilean took us for some pizza, and to see home alone and then to friendlys. He didn't want a funeral so that night we went to see him before he went away. I bought some flowers for him and I used all of my money and I'm still broke. And when I was born he said thank god it's another girl the army can't take her away.

I am haunted by the sentence near the end—"I bought some flowers for him and I used all of my money and I'm still broke"—which seems to have layers of meaning the young writer is unaware of, particularly with the use of the word "broke." A mentor can highlight such fortunate accidents for the young writer.

A mentor builds on strengths, often seeing more in a student's work than the student sees. One day Robert Cohen, friend and author of *The Organ Builder,* said to me:

"The lines in your poem have lots of energy. Texture. The lines are dense. But in your prose writing the sentences tend to be flatter, smoother, more transparent. If I were you I'd try to put more of the dense, textured language that's in your poetry into your prose."

This advice literally changed me as a writer. But it could only have been given by someone who knew my work well. And it was easy to take because he prefaced his suggestion by first commenting on what he perceived as a strength in my writing.

A MENTOR VALUES ORIGINALITY AND DIVERSITY

Recently I watched Artie Voigt, a staff developer in Brooklyn, New York, work with fifteen young Long Island writers during a two-week writing institute for children and teachers.

"Is your class coming together?" one teacher asked him.

"I don't *want* them to come together," Artie replied. "I want the kids to keep going in whatever direction they need to go."

A writing teacher will challenge students to attain a species of excellence according to particular beliefs about writing. This cannot be otherwise; it's hard to teach what you don't believe. The teacher, however, may encounter a student whose writing differs dramatically from the teacher's idea of excellent writing. A true mentor will not try to penalize the student or clone a duplicate of himself. Rather, the mentor is forever alive to the possibility of something new and distinctly original.

Anne, a teacher I work with, wrote a series of stories when she was in fifth grade. The teacher read them and, realizing that she didn't quite know what to do with them, passed them on to a local author. The author telephoned Anne.

"Did this all really happen?" the author asked.

"No," Anne admitted. "I made most of it up."

"Well, you're the best damn liar I've ever come across," the author retorted. "Keep writing!"

A mentor possesses an inner honesty, an ability to recognize that the novice's different style of writing may camouflage a deeper truth: The novice writes better than the teacher. It requires courage and real humility to recognize this and step graciously out of the way.

"That's the most humbling thing about teaching," one teacher told me mournfully. "You teach some kids who are just plain smarter—some of them a *lot* smarter—than you are."

A MENTOR ENCOURAGES STUDENTS TO TAKE RISKS

A kindergarten teacher is preparing her children for a visit to a dinosaur exhibit.

"What do you think 'extinct' means?" she asks.

"I think it means the dinosaurs *smelled,*" one boy says. "You know, like *stink.*"

"No," the teacher replies with a big grin, "but that's smart thinking. That's a great guess, Ron!"

"Wait, I think I know," the same boy says. "It's *ex*-tinct, so it must mean that the dinosaurs *don't* smell. Right?"

"Ron, that is so smart!" the teacher says to him.

This teacher places a higher value on Ron's habits of thought, his willingness to apply his knowledge to brand new information, than she does on his getting the correct answer.

Risk, as Patrick Shannon points out, is crucially important: Risk allows children to outgrow themselves. But schools today don't go nearly far enough to encourage students to take risks in their learning. Compare Ron to the fourth-grade girl who runs up to her teacher waving a paper back and forth, asking: "Is this poem right or is it wrong?"

Any writer who labors under such a right/wrong schema will never allow herself the fluency and playfulness, the time and perseverance she will need over the long haul to become a skillful writer.

Novice writers often go through a great deal of turmoil, an era of rich experimentation, before attaining any degree of confidence as a writer. This may include physically copying a short story out of a book, attempting a free verse poem instead of a rhyming couplet, playing with various leads, aping the style of a favorite writer, free-writing, using longer sentences, trying out a more complex vocabulary.

It's important to recognize the critical place this kind of experimentation has in the writer's development. The mentor will not penalize the student whose risks do not immediately produce a superbly written essay or report. We need to redefine the success ethic, not just in writing classes but during the entire school day, to mean not only "Did you get it right?" but also "Did you take a chance? Did you try something you've never tried before?"

A MENTOR IS PASSIONATE

Passion remains the most important quality the mentor has to offer. When we think back on those teachers we looked up to, we don't always remember exactly what they taught. Above everything, we remember passion. Fire.

At Dartmouth, I took Peter Bien's course that compared James Joyce and Nikos Kazantzakis. On the last day of the class Bien, a balding, bespectacled man and leading authority on Kazantzakis, put down his notes and spoke to us directly, ending with a plea that we all "keep reading, keep buying books." He stopped. We looked at the clock: time was up. The course was over. All seventy students stood up spontaneously and gave him a rousing ovation. What were we cheering about, anyway? Not his sense of humor, which was fine, if a bit dry. Not his scholarship, which was impeccable. We were relishing this man's passion for ideas.

After watching his daughter Susannah learn how to sail, Artie Voigt commented to me: "It's such a great feeling to watch someone else enjoying what you love to do yourself." Through the relationship with a novice, the mentor gets to experience the thrill of the craft (as well as its pain) all over again. In this way the mentor's passion never gets spent: it gets renewed again and again through the mentoring relationship.

A MENTOR LOOKS AT THE BIG PICTURE

All writers have off-days, get bored, get silly, get blocked, get derivative, get lazy, "borrow" sentences. Take the long view.

I learned an important idea about teaching writing while preparing for the birth of my son. In our childbirth class, our teacher had this suggestion for husbands (and writing teachers) who are nervous about doing and saying the right thing at the critical moment. Relax, she told us. Try to remember that *tenderness is more important than technique.*

Even the most skilled young writers can absorb only a certain amount of this fire, a limited amount of direct instruction, at any given time. We need to be patient: The fuse we light is a slow-burning one.

More important, we need to be gentle. Raymond Carver, writer and teacher, was revered by his students. The harshest criticism he would give to a student was: "I think it's good you got that story behind you."

Moments after Robert was born, his tight purple I-can't-believe-this-is-happening-to-me face quickly dissolved into howls. A very loud howling indeed. I looked apprehensively at the midwife. She was smiling broadly.

"Do you see how strong his lungs and voice are?" she asked. "Remarkable!"

Minutes later Robert was being weighed, checked, and taking his first standardized test, the APGAR. I was astonished to see him hoist a tiny fist up to his mouth and begin sucking noisily.

"Look at that!" the midwife said, grinning. "Look at how well he's able to take care of himself!"

I looked at JoAnn. Amazing! It had *looked* like he was howling in distress. It had *seemed* like he was merely sucking his fists. But that midwife helped me see it differently. And I expanded into the way she saw it. Strong lungs and voice. Yes, that's my robust little boy. Remarkable how he's able to take care of himself even as a tiny infant. I swelled with pride.

As a new father, I was wholly dependent on the midwife's appraisal of my newborn son. In the same way, young writers are deeply vulnerable to teachers' appraisals of their stories, poems, or essays. We must speak to our students with an honesty tempered by compassion: Our words will literally define the ways they perceive themselves as writers.

TWO
Freezing to the Face

Writing is easy. You just sit at the typewriter and open a vein.
RED SMITH

I ONCE VISITED an art fair where one exhibit in particular caught my eye: a series of sculptures constructed entirely from automobile transmissions pulled from abandoned cars. The artist had twisted them into marvelously expressive shapes: a crane, a man, even an enormous double-humped camel. At the entrance to the exhibit a plaque was hanging (burnt letters in maple) that said: ART IS THE TRANSMISSION OF DISCOVERY.

Yes! And the saying seems just as applicable to the act of writing. Many people still assume that most writers bring a mental text that is more or less assembled when they encounter a blank piece of paper. Writing would seem to be merely a matter of transcribing onto paper what already exists in the mind. Right?

Wrong. Research on writing, and the words of writers themselves, suggest a far stranger, far less logical writing process than that. Less neat. It turns out that many writers actually discover what they have to say in the process of writing it. The writer's challenge is to keep this sense of discovery intact; this keeps writing fresh and vibrant.

I discussed this notion of writing-as-discovery recently with a junior high teacher who insisted his students outline everything before they wrote it. He interrupted angrily.

"Come on," he said. "Are you kidding? Listen, let me ask you a question. Would you ever get on a bus if you didn't know where it was going? Would you?"

In such situations, I'm always torn between answering the rhetorical question or trying to address the hostility behind it. At that moment all I could do was stammer that writing and riding a bus are not the same thing and should not be approached as if they were identical.

But the more I thought about it the more it occurred to me that there is more than one way of riding a bus. True, riding a bus can be a simple matter of getting from here to there. But riding a bus (writing) can also be a way of *exploring* a new place (subject). Many times in Dublin, in Paris, or in the Caribbean, I boarded buses without knowing their exact destination. I simply rode around until I found a neighborhood that struck my fancy. A slice of the city was what I hungered for—that was the only *there* I was after. I still find this a terrific way of exploring a new place. In time you begin to notice landmarks, you begin to get a feel for the territory. You can always get off and get on a new bus anytime you feel like it.

Marilyn Jody, professor of English at Western Carolina University and an important mentor of mine, likes to tell this anecdote about mountain climbing. While scaling a sheer rock face, mountain climbers face a dilemma that forces them to act in a way that is counter-intuitive and would seem to go against all common sense. For a moment, a mountain climber must let go of whatever perch he has secured to reach to the next higher place. There is no way around it. A climber who is too frightened to let go finds himself "frozen to the face," literally unable to move. He hangs there, paralyzed. Finally, when his strength gives out, he falls.

It's hard not to see this story as a parable for many moments in life: loving, learning/teaching, and writing. Writers of all ages face myriad subtle temptations to "freeze to the face" by writing something safely mainstream and formulaic. F. Scott Fitzgerald and Raymond Chandler were tempted by lucrative monetary contracts to write for the screen instead of writing novels. (Faulkner and Steinbeck did write screenplays and were extremely disappointed in the outcome.) The same thing often happens in classrooms. Students learn to find out what a teacher expects and write to those expectations—and the accompanying grades—instead of trying to internalize their own high standards for writing.

When I was twenty-one I sat down to write a novel. What did it matter that my life until that point had not been, as I freely admitted to myself, all that remarkable? My novelistic options seemed limited to three choices—college years, my family, and a half-serious love affair—all of which were still too recent to afford me the benefit of any real perspective or reflective wisdom. But I didn't know that, and I wouldn't have cared if I had known. I was determined to write a novel, and concocted a plot suitable enough for this purpose.

I began by making a serious outline. This took nearly two weeks. Every chapter got outlined right down to the small a. and b. I wrote my novel the way I figured all writers wrote: by carefully following this outline. No matter what idea came into my head—a possible new complication, some unforeseen digression or tantalizing character flaw—I pushed it aside if it did not appear on the original outline.

The result, of course, was disastrous: a stiff, lifeless work. Stillborn. I had frozen to the face of my outline and never allowed myself to take advantage of any startling little surprises that came up along the way. My novel was not a transmission of discovery because the outline did not allow for discovery, at least not the way I used it.

Writing process has helped demystify the act of writing. But maybe we need to *remystify* it. We have heard that clear writing comes from clear thinking. William Zinsser, among others, has exhorted us to write strong, uncluttered prose. Teachers of writing have worked hard to learn and teach the "writing logic" that would help students to write well. Skilled writing would seem to be similar to building a house. The writer needs material, a blueprint, and elbow grease to finish the project. Simple, isn't it?

But it's not that simple. When I write I am always struck at how complex, magical, illogical, and unexpected the process turns out to be. Take the writing of this book. For many months I gathered information in my accordion file on leads, endings, voice, sense of place, characterization. I assumed that these would become chapters in the book.

But when I began writing, the first chapter was called "Mentors," which was not one of the original sections in my accordion file. An aberration, perhaps. The next chapter, this one, had "Risk" as its working title. The chapter after that one was titled "Words"; I was surprised to discover that I had a lot of ideas about this subject. None of these chapters were part of the book as I originally conceived it. My book began evolving into something very different from what I'd imagined. The new chapters, less practical, more theoretical, confused me. What's going on? I wondered. Should I return to my original outline? I would have done so if this new material did not seem so absorbing. Compelled, if disoriented, I pushed ahead.

Do you know this story? A little girl watches a sculptor at work. He begins carving into a large wooden cube and works hard all day. By late afternoon, the shape of a lion has begun to emerge. Absolutely dumbfounded, the little girl looks at the sculptor and sputters, "But how did you know there was a lion inside that wood?"

The writer experiences the same kind of childlike disbelief each time a story/poem/novel/essay begins to take shape. And this is a major part of the risk writers undertake—never knowing exactly what's going to turn up on the page. Everything changes when you allow your writing to be influenced and shaped by discoveries made during the process of writing. Your narrative is suddenly not as safe and predictable as you might have thought. You swim across the river and find yourself far downstream of wherever it was you hoped you'd end up. You discover that your topic has a hidden trapdoor leading down into a dusty underbarn you would have preferred to stay out of. You start writing about an antique table your grandmother owned, but before you know it you are writing about the thrill and shame of a secret romance you had with your first cousin, a girl who didn't look and seem the least bit like a blood relative. You begin writing about getting your allowance every Saturday morning and find yourself writing about that stack of new twenty dollar bills you found when you were twelve years old under your father's sweaters in the bottom drawer of his dresser . . .

No, skilled writers don't meander off the topic every chance they get. They don't entertain every whim that comes into their heads. The writer must find a middle ground between this kind of free writing and the rigid way I wrote my first novel. A writer may find a creative tension springing up between the original vision of the writing and how it turns out. But the temptation will always exist to take the safe way out—to cling stubbornly to the cliff.

Among the many hidden traps the writer must circumnavigate, *success*, and the deceptive safety it seems to provide, may be the most insidious trap of all.

During college I spent a day helping a very old and retired obstetrician plant five hundred pine saplings. I was touched by the quiet heroism of this act—planting trees that would never grant him shade—and a few years later I wrote a short story about it. I sent it off to *Redbook*. They promptly accepted it, agreed to pay me $400, and published it in their Christmas edition. This success had a galvanizing effect on my shaky confidence: the cold cash, the millions of readers, being published in the same issue as Ray Bradbury. On an airplane, in February, I met a young woman from Albuquerque who had read the story and who flattered me with her praise. My spirits soared.

All of this was wonderful, except that now I was hooked. I wanted to be a writer for *Redbook*. I wanted my stories to be smiled at by young mothers over their morning coffee in Albuquerque, Anchorage, Aspen, Atlanta . . . I wanted to be on the *inside* for a change. I had paid my dues, hadn't I? And for two years I tried to replicate this early success. I mailed a steady stream of stories to *Redbook*—all of them wholesome, poignant, saleable. Awful. After *Redbook* rejected them, I sent them off to other magazines, and then to others. I began plastering rejection notices on the wall above my desk. It was not until five years later that I could clearly see how I'd frozen to this particular face: I had poisoned the voice in my writing by trying at all cost to be a popular magazine writer.

Students can fall into a similar trap, a trap set by us if we're not careful. We praise a student for trying an auditory lead ("Clomp! Clomp! Clomp! My brother thundered down the stairs . . ."). But now all her writings begin with sound effects as she pursues additional praise.

In a sixth-grade classroom, I watched a boy try to work on a second draft of a story he had written. He sat slumped and dispirited while I tried to talk with him.

"Do you really want to do a second draft on this?" I asked. "Why don't you put it away and work on a new story?"

"I'd like to," he said, "but Mrs. C gave me a B- on this first draft. She says if I work harder I can pull it up to an A-. I have to add more description and details. That's the kind of writing she likes."

This is one of the ways we sabotage our students as risk-takers. The cost runs high when we coerce students (through grades, praise, favoritism), however subtly, to shoehorn their emerging language into the narrow parameters we set for what constitutes "good writing" in our classrooms. Writing teachers need to ask ourselves some hard questions. How can we encourage students to internalize their own high standards for writing? Are we willing to allow these standards to differ from our own?

In Tom Robbins's wonderful novel *Even Cowgirls Get the Blues*, the author quips that "the only difference between a vacation and an adventure is the margin of safety." Writing is no vacation. On many different levels, the writer faces a shaved margin of safety if not outright danger: the danger of being misunderstood, ridiculed. The danger of failure. The danger of rejection. I had one poem rejected a dozen years ago by an editor who wrote back: "Bad, bad, compares with your prose." I still have that rejection. It still hurts.

A writer becomes vulnerable by revealing part of her inner life. This is the fine print in the reader-writer agreement: When we read, we expect to learn about the writer and, through the writer, about ourselves.

Writing with real honesty takes tremendous courage. Such writing should never be taken for granted; writers of all ages often find that they lack the nerve to write honestly. Factors of environment may figure into this—not simply the classroom environment but also the insidious effects of television.

In *The Art of Fiction,* John Gardner says: "Much of the dialogue one encounters in student fiction, as well as plot, gesture, even setting, come not from life but from life filtered through tv. Many student writers seem unable to tell their most important stories—the death of a father, the first disillusionment of love—except in terms of tv. And . . . tv is false to life."

Writing teachers cannot unplug students' tv sets, but we can watch for and celebrate the appearance of honest writing. In the poem in Figure 2–1, Jane, a third grader, speaks through the mask of being a penny.

Brandon, a fourth grader, wrote this poem. Brandon's two metaphors follow hard upon each other, but the turbulence of the mixed metaphors helps to create the poem's undeniable power.

> *Adopted*
>
> I was almost like picked out of a hat,
> Being adopted feels something like that,
> It's like going on a rollercoaster,
> Landing with the wrong parents.

I had the privilege of actually watching Francesca, a Long Island third grader, write this story:

HOW MY FAMILY CHANGED

My dad died when I was two months old. He died in a car accident. He was driving home from work. He was rushed to the hospital. By the time my mom got there the doctor told my mom he was dead. My mom told me all she could think about was me. How I would feel when I got older. One time my mom said: "You could have taken a bath in my tears, Francesca."

I don't feel great but I don't feel terrible that my father died. My mom is seeing someone who I was not crazy about at first. But now I like the man. His name is Joe. He is real nice. I decided to share my feelings with other children who have stories similar to mine so I joined a group called "Banana Splits." I feel so much better now that I know I can share my feelings with other kids. I can even talk with my mom. I love her.

This young writer explores the most basic questions of all: Who am I? What is my history and how did it begin? As teachers we take a risk ourselves when we allow students to choose their own subjects, particularly when they decide to write about issues that make us uneasy.

The best writing classes I visit are taught by teachers who work hard at creating an environment where children can put themselves on the line when they write. They do this by reading out loud the books and poems that powerfully affect them; students tune in to the emotion in their voices. They read accessible examples of literature dealing with risky issues (see Appendix). They share some of the resonant issues in their own lives. They

A Penny

Found in the gutter,
All wet,
Someone picks me
up,
Hugs me in there
hand,
All sweaty, Spent
At the
Candy store I was
Being
Exchanged for a
Piece
Of candy I wasn't
Loved
I was picked up
For
A peice of candy
I wasn't
Going to be kept
Because
I was special. I'm
Not anymore
I'm in a cash register
by- Jane

Figure 2-1

write and share their writing—especially the false starts, the writing that doesn't work—with their students. When I teach writing, I often start by talking about ideas I might write about:

- Getting lost at the circus when I was seven
- Haunted house (on Block Island, Rhode Island)
- "Third Parent": being the oldest of nine children
- The last kiss
- Leaving for college
- Bobby's death

I find it helpful to divide this list into two categories—safe topics and risky topics. I suspect I could skate through fairly safe topics such as "haunted house" and "lost at the circus," though I would not expect to make any big discoveries about myself through the writing. I would rather take my chances on the thinner, though possibly richer, ice of a subject that is more unresolved.

THE LAST KISS

If it had nothing else, my childhood had symmetry. Teeth brushed morning and night. Good deeds and sin. The bus to school and the bus back home. My mother and my father. Chores and play, light and dark, inside and out. Ale's Woods and the mowed grass of our lawn.

This symmetry seemed pervasive, an apparent law of nature. It extended to the kisses I got from my parents just before bed. First, my mother. At bedtime I would come to where she stood washing dishes, wiping the table, or, rarely, resting on the couch with her feet up.

"My poor dogs are barking," she'd sigh, smiling and leaning forward. To me, at least, our kisses were passionate moments that passed much too quickly. I was the oldest. She was the first woman I ever loved. A goodnight kiss from my mother meant a great big hug, as well; I learned that this was one way to extend the experience. Her cheek was smooth and soft. I walked away with the good, honest, hardworking smell of my mother's skin—along with the faint cigarette smokiness of her hair—in my nostrils.

All this happened in a matter of seconds. My mother's kisses contained potent medicine to ward off spirits of the night, but not potent enough. I was grateful to go next to my father. His goodnight kisses were more formal affairs, but that was all right. Formality was exactly what I wanted just before bed. And no accompanying body hug, either. Just this: his male scent, the faintest remnants of morning aftershave lotion, and the whisker-stubbly contour of his proffered cheek—a textured surface that made a satisfying contrast with my mother's cheek. Kissing my tall, handsome father always imbued me with a strong dose of masculine courage. Thus blessed, twice-kissed, I could go off safely to bed.

This arrangement worked very well indeed and lasted through kindergarten, first grade, and into second grade. It was such an intrinsic part of my childhood—like making my bed or saying my prayers—that I never bothered to question it.

One night I went to kiss my mother goodnight. Mom was bottle-feeding the eternal Fletcher baby (Joey? Kathy?) at the time; I had to lean over the little one to get to my mother. She let the baby cradle on her lap while she kissed and hugged me. It was from embraces like this one that I would learn a first crucial rule of affection: Important kisses always take place with the eyes closed. In my case, the better to feel her strong arms, her warmth. The better to concentrate on her smell: perfume, dishwashing lotion, and the smell that was simply her.

Next I went to find my father. He was working down in the basement; he glanced up at me when I approached. My father knew exactly why I was there, but on this evening he became busy and commenced to energetically beat the dust out of some window screens with a whisk broom. I watched him for a while, tapping my foot, trying to be patient. Several minutes passed.

"I'm going to bed, Dad," I said at last.

"Well, good night, then," he said, giving me a kind of half-smile, half-sigh that was peculiar to him. I was stunned. There was something in his voice that made me decide not to ask again.

I went to bed. Outside, sounds of the summer night: crickets, a sprinkler hissing, some neighborhood kids still playing, the ice-cream truck taunting kids with its twilight ringing.

Next night I decided to try my father again. Maybe last night's missed kiss was no more than a quirk. I went to him first this time and found him outside, behind his car, the trunk opened, sorting through book samples he would need to make his sales call the next day. He was on the road a great deal; it was not unusual for him to be gone all week. It was nearly 8:30 and the lawn behind him was alive with fireflies. They drifted through the cool twilight like bits of phosphorescent jellyfish in the tide. I approached him noisily, clearing my throat, shuffling my feet.

"It's bed time," I murmured. I wonder, now, if he heard only those words or also the plea behind it, the desire for clarification. Maybe it was no more than the sound of quiet expectancy a child makes when he says: "I'm hungry." I don't know. I merely watched with sinking heart as my father's hands got busy again, not with me but with something else, this time stacking his book samples in cardboard boxes. He stood up and turned to me. He reached forward to touch my arm. He squeezed my shoulder.

"Good night, then," he said, turning away. I stood there a moment, while the fireflies pulsed in silence. I was eight years old. The thought my mind held was too large to formulate into a question, too vague to clearly recognize as loss.

It took several more nights, several more awkward tries, before the grim truth finally sunk in. I was too old to be kissed by my father. True, I could go to my mother and get a huge bearhug along with a kiss. But now that the smoothness of her cheek was not counterbalanced by my father's fine sandpaper, even her kisses felt different, not nearly so powerful, much more fragile. I would never again embrace her without some part of me wondering if I might not one day lose her kisses, as well.

THREE
A Love of Words

Language permits us to see. Without the word, we are all blind.
CARLOS FUENTES, *The Old Gringo*

STRANGE OCCURRENCES. In November I took a group of kids to the Bronx Zoo. We reached the buffaloes and stopped to admire the immense bulk, the shaggy shredding coats.

"Buffaloes!" a little boy said, and I felt a stab of pure emotion, sharp, bittersweet.

"C'mon, let's go," another kid said. But I couldn't move. Buffaloes. The word reverberated oddly inside my head. I was dazed, rooted to the spot. I was actually on the brink of tears. Yet I couldn't quite bring it to the surface, that deep memory fragment. I shook it off and all but forgot it. But on the way home from the zoo the kids started singing "Home on the Range," and when they got to the part "where the buffaloes roam" there it was again— pungent emotion, pure and sad and sweet, surging up inside me.

Months passed. One day I was hanging up JoAnn's white bathrobe and just like that the memory came flooding back. Dad's bathrobe. When I was little, for some reason (the shaggy bulk?) we always called Dad's bathrobe his "buffalo." He traveled a lot during those years, selling books all over New England. The first thing he did when he came home on Friday night was to don slippers and that big white terrycloth bathrobe. We would snuggle hard against that buffalo while he read stories to us before bed.

Some nights during the week while Dad was away we would start pestering my mother. Couldn't we take Dad's buffalo out of his closet? Just for a little while? If she agreed, we'd race upstairs to the closet in his bedroom. The buffalo always hung on a particular hook; we would jostle each other to be first to pull it down. The buffalo got dragged downstairs to the living room where we would wrap it around us while we watched tv. It was so big that two or even three kids could nestle within its white bulk. Beyond its warmth and softness, the most wonderful thing about the robe was how it had soaked up Dad's essence, his *smell.* We would sit there, wrapped in the warmth and comforting scent of the father we missed so much. I discovered that if I closed my eyes it was nearly possible to believe that he really was there himself, holding us in his strong arms.

Today the word *buffalo* sounds to me like power commingled with regret: the mighty beasts that were all but wiped out as white America moved west. But also a deeper and more personal regret tangled up with missing my father.

Artists develop a love for the feel of their tools, the smell and texture of clay, wood, or paint. My brother Jim has imported ebony all the way from Nigeria for some of his most memorable sculptures. The lithographer Tanya Grosman searched the world to find paper of astonishing beauty and rarity to lure artists such as Jasper Johns, Larry Rivers, Buckminster Fuller, and Robert Rauschenburg to her Universal Limited Art Editions studio in West Islip, New York.

Writers are no different. Writers love words. And while some writers get excited over a particular pen or a more powerful word processing program, words remain the most important tool the writer has to work with.

"If you want to write and you're not in love with your language, you shouldn't be writing," Jane Yolen says bluntly. "Words are the writer's tools."

"When I write," Cynthia Rylant says, "my mind's not filled with visual imagery. It's filled with language. Words. I seek words, I chase after them. When I write I'm trying to put the most beautiful words in the world down on paper."

Not all writers work like Rylant; some writers do begin with images, others with emotion. Either way the writer must use words to communicate the story/image/emotion. Writers obsess over words, their origins, their sounds. Writers have pet words, favorite and worst words, words imbued with other associations and personal meanings. In *One Writer's Beginnings*, Eudora Welty describes the sensual awareness she developed of particular words such as moon: "The word 'moon' comes into my mouth as though fed to me out of a silver spoon. Held in my mouth the moon became a word. It had the roundness of a Concord grape Grandpa took off his vine and gave me to suck out of its skin and swallow whole, in Ohio."

Writers love their language, but the language they love may not be a conventional tongue. Mark Twain's many books captured the colorful vernacular of the Mississippi region. Eloise Greenfield is one of many African-American writers to use Black English for her sparkling book of poems,

Honey, I Love. And Darrell H.Y. Lum, a Hawaiian writer, uses a rich and musical pidgin English in a short story like "The Moiliili Bag Man." The language used by a writer may be powerful or lyrically beautiful even while it does not conform to conventional grammar.

The writer's fascination with words has roots in the child's natural play with language. In late May of 1989, my friend Jenifer Hall took a trip up north with her daughter, Emma. Jenifer explained that they were going to see Ralph and JoAnn get married in Ludlow, Vermont. Emma, who was about twenty months old at the time, fell instantly in love with that word: Ludlow. For two solid hours she sang and chanted and played with its sounds: "Lud-low, lud-low . . . lud-lud-lud and low-low-low . . . LUD-low LUD-low, LUD-low-low-low-low . . . luddy-luddy-luddy-lud . . . luddy-luddy-luddy-low . . ."

"Read like a wolf eats," Gary Paulsen says to young readers, and as a boy I did that. I was a ravenous reader, and it didn't take long to figure out that each new word brought you into a whole new room, with new views and distinct intellectual furniture. The Boy Scout Oath's lofty aims ("trust-worthy, loyal, helpful, friendly, courteous, kind, obedient, cheerful, thrifty, brave, clean, and reverent") were counterbalanced by less pure descriptors such as *voluptuous,* and *callipygean*—exotic and barely under-stood words I first encountered in books, words that took on sultry new nuances as I moved into adolescence.

One sweltering summer day, while my young father struggled to mow the lawn with a hand mower, I was sitting with my best friend on the porch. He confided to me the worst swear in the world. Only nine years old, I watched from a safe distance my father mop sweat off his forehead while my friend whispered the muggy monosyllabic word, softly, so my father would not hear. It seemed monstrous that such a word could co-exist juxtaposed (another of my favorite words) against the image of my saintly, toiling father. Swears amazed me. "Duck" was perfectly all right, but if your mother heard you rhyme that word with another word only two letters after the "D" you could get your mouth washed out with soap.

Another amazing thing: Words could mean different things at different times. The spoken word "see" might also mean "sea"—or even the letter "C." Many words contained delightful shades of ambiguity. When I was five I loved to play with homonyms: "bear" and "bare," "red" and "read." This early language play would later blossom in a poem like "Waves" (from *Water Planet*):

Waves on the ocean,
Ripples on the sand,
My father calling me
With a wave of his hand.

The wavy grain of wood,
The wave in my hair,
Waves of fiery autumn leaves
Tumbling through the air.

A wave of sadness
When I think of the way
My best friend Vinnie
Moved far far away.

I grew up in Brant Rock, Massachusetts, where there was a fabulous candy store: Buds. Once a week, if we were lucky, my mother would walk us down to Buds, where the bins and counters were crammed with chocolate cigarettes and bubblegum cigars, red wax lips and black wax mustaches, dots and red hots, jaw-breakers and ju-ju beads . . . Many of the candies were priced two or even three for a penny; if you shopped wisely you could end up with a whole bag of sweets for a nickel or a dime.

At that time *bamboozled* and *flabbergasted* were my favorite words. I loved the feel of those words in my mouth, and still cannot conjure them up except in terms of taste. *Bamboozled* has a fizzly Sweet Tart taste that begins in a rush of sweetness but always ends with a tingly, tickly feeling at the top of the mouth. *Flabbergasted,* on the other hand, tastes and sounds as nutty as a Heath Bar.

I kept a mental list of my favorite words, some of which I loved for the odd pictures they made in my mind, others merely for their exotic sounds: *babushka, cockatoo, pumpernickel,* and *periwinkle.* Later I would keep actual lists of words and trade them with similarly inclined friends. (We were not necessarily the most popular kids in the school.) Each word carried its own peculiar kind of melody. While words like *umber, mellow, sonorous,* and *quiescent* sounded soothing, words like *obstreperous, truculent, vituper-ative,* and *obdurate* seemed to jut their very chins out at the world.

The Fletcher family was a den of rabid Boston Bruin hockey fans. Back then the Bruins had a few future Hall of Fame players, like Phil Esposito and Bobby Orr. Otherwise, the team consisted primarily of players who hustled, checked hard, and enjoyed fighting, or appeared to, at least. The Bruins were forever getting into brawls. I was an avid reader of the *Boston Globe* sports section, and it was great fun trying to envision the sports writers thumbing through their thesauruses in search of new words for these nightly altercations. My siblings and I roared over the words they came up with: *imbroglio, fisticuffs, slugfest, donnybrook,* and (my favorite) *brouhaha.*

In high school, while other kids admired teachers with the best looks, biggest muscles, or fastest cars, I admired those teachers with the most remarkable vocabularies. Mr. Thompson and Mr. Plumer were able to take words like *perspicacious, noumenous,* or even *contemporaneous* and weave them seamlessly into their lectures. I would copy down the words and race home to look them up.

Fancy words like *perspicacious* were one thing. But sometimes, I discovered two ordinary words placed next to each other could wake up and create an effect that went far beyond the capabilities of either one. This is exactly what led to my deciding to title my first book *Walking Trees,* taken from a conversation I had with a first-grade girl. Put together, these two words try to pull each other in opposite directions. The phrase *walking trees* embodies a concept almost impossible to put in words: paradox, when two opposing ideas can both be true at the same time.

In the early 1960s, my siblings and I roamed through the thick pine woods around our house in Marshfield, Massachusetts. My brother Jim was a born naturalist, with vacuum eyes that sucked up incredible treasures during his long solitary treks through the woods. Every single day he would bring home some unusual insect, snake, or turtle he had found.

One day, after a bad windstorm, Jim and I were walking through a swampy part of the woods. A tree had fallen in the storm; a shallow pool had formed in the crater left by the huge mass of uplifted roots. At the edge of the water we saw something lurch into the water, a kind of lizard we had never seen before. We got just the briefest glimpse of red before the creature disappeared.

"Didya see that?"

"It looked some kind of newt," I said. "A salamander."

"That was no salamander," Jim said. "Didn't you see the red on its gills?"

Jim went home and proceeded to pull out several volumes of the World Book Encyclopaedia. For two hours he sat poring through volumes A (amphibians), L (lizard), and R (reptiles).

"I found it," he said, showing me a picture. "A mud puppy. That's definitely it. We saw a mud puppy. They're common around here, found in the swamps, rivers, and lakes of northeastern America. Their external gills are bright red."

Mud puppy! I fell in love with the odd name, the internal rhyme, the funny image it forced into my head. The name clicked. By the end of that week all the kids in the neighborhood were calling the swampy area near that uprooted tree Mud Puppy Place.

Journal entry, January 30, 1991. JoAnn is studying for the GREs. Three hundred core words for the vocabulary section. Stacks of vocabulary cards in the bathroom. Big, cocky, multisyllabic words. Abstemious, convivial, concatenation. These words strut around the house, loud and arrogant. Worse, they have actually shouldered their way into our spoken sentences.

"Don't you think the war is *reprehensible?*"

"Don't *prevaricate*. The point is that when it comes to contributions, some of our allies certainly haven't been very *munificent.*"

These words are obnoxious, but we cater to them. At least for now, we need them far more than they need us.

Words are the writer's primal tools. But anyone who tries to write English—child or adult—immediately gets caught in a kind of linguistic stranglehold that makes it difficult to use those tools. Our English language contains about 490,000 words, along with another 300,000 technical terms. No one, of course, not even the great writers, can utilize so much richness. It has been said that Shakespeare had a working vocabulary of around 33,000 words. In 1945, the average American student between the ages of six and fourteen had a written vocabulary of 25,000 words. Today, that vocabulary has shrunk to about 10,000 words.

The mass media has helped to further tighten this noose. Popular print media draw from a small group of words; television, of course, draws from the smallest word pool of all. The implications for this stranglehold go far beyond the dangers of falling SAT scores.

It seems to me that the first step toward breaking this linguistic stranglehold is for teachers to model our own curiosity with words. Recently I decided to bring a bag of words into the schools where I work as a writing consultant. I wanted to let kids know how crucial words are to me as a writer. But how to proceed? I was surer about what I *didn't* want to do. I knew I didn't want to turn it into a vocabulary lesson, carefully disguised instruction on roots or suffixes, or an exercise in using the dictionary.

I walked into a fifth-grade classroom and began by writing some of my favorite words on the blackboard. Some were funny sounding words: *persnickety*, *oxymoron*, and *troglodyte* (which the students especially liked for its usefulness in insulting people). I had chosen several small words for their sheer potency: *triage, quisling, quietas.*

Kids started scrambling for the dictionaries. It turned out, however, that the school-use dictionaries in the classroom didn't house most of the words I had brought in with me. I sent a student down to the library. A few minutes later he returned, grunting under the weight of Webster's monstrous 2,347-page 320,000-word *New Universal Unabridged Dictionary.* We were in business.

Mnemonic. Touchstone. Onomatopoeia. The kids were delighted to learn that *fontanel* is the word for the soft spot at the top of a baby's head. Next, I scribbled on the board several truly bizarre words:

jirble—a craving for unnatural food, such as dust
geniophobia—fear of chins
xenoglossy—understanding a language one has never learned

"Probably the longest word in the English language is *pneumonoultra-microscopicsilicovolcanoconiosis,*" I told the students. "Forty-five letters. It's a kind of lung disease miners can get."

The kids howled, impressed that I knew what it meant and could actually pronounce it. The asked me to say it several more times, and insisted I write in the board.

"How about you?" I asked. "Do you have any favorite words?"

"I've always liked *plummet,*" one boy said. "I like the way it sounds."

"I like *tintinnabulation,*" one girl said, pronouncing the word perfectly. "It means the ringing of the bells."

I wrote down their words: *déjà vu, exposé, deciduous.*

"I like the word *mistress,*" one very tall girl said. "I mean, I don't like what it means but I like how it sounds." She paused and looked at me with narrowed eyes. "What *does* it mean?"

I glanced at the fifth-grade teacher. The teacher answered quickly, casually, as if she had been expecting the question.

"Mistress is one of those words with more than one meaning," she explained. "Mistress can be a proper title for a woman. And it can also be the word for a woman who goes out with a married man."

"Oh," the girl said.

Jane Yolen describes three different vocabularies: a reading vocabulary, a writing vocabulary, and a speaking vocabulary. "There are some words that are wonderful but they're reading words only, or writing words—not speaking words," Yolen says. "And those of us who are writers also have a secret vocabulary."

My secret vocabulary includes words I often save for a long time, several years, until I can actually use them in a piece of writing. I hoarded _postprandial_ (an adjective meaning "after dinner," as in "postprandial coffee") for no less than five years and was thrilled to actually be able to use the word in my first book. Another secret word of mine is _gegenschein_—a faint, glowing spot in the sky exactly opposite the position of the sun; also called "counterglow." I have kept this word for a long, long time; I'm not at all sure I shall ever find a legitimate place to use it in a sentence. Still, it's good to have such a word around in case the need arises.

A rich vocabulary allows a writer to get a richness of thought onto the paper. However, the writer's real pleasure comes not from using an exotic word but from using the _right_ word in a sentence. Not long ago, while writing an article, I labored over this sentence: "Many school districts are finding it difficult to _____ a whole-language approach with existing reading programs, which rely heavily on basals."

I could not think of the missing word. But I knew it was out there—the single word that would make the sentence click, make its meaning snap into instant focus. It had something to do with paradox, with linking two things that don't quite go together. _Juxtapose_ was close, but it wasn't the right word. I kept plugging other, less precise words into the sentence and rereading to see how it sounded. Link? No. Equate? No. Compare? Bridge? Nope. Finally, I gave up and moved to another part of the article.

That night, in bed, I suddenly opened my eyes. Sat bolt upright.

"RECONCILE!" I said to JoAnn.

"Huh?"

"Reconcile!" I grinned at her. "The word I've been looking for. 'School districts are finding it difficult to _reconcile_ a whole-language approach with existing reading programs, which rely heavily on basals.' Eureka!"

As teachers, we can share with students the pleasure in finding the precise word to communicate a nuance of thought. We can encourage students to play naturally with language. And we can celebrate their language breakthroughs wherever and whenever they occur. After reading _Charlotte's Web_, Donna, a third grader, told her teacher: "I think I want to use the word _perish_ in my story instead of _die_."

Is _perish_ a better word than _die_? Not necessarily. Not always. Often a simple word is better than the fancy word. But in this case Donna took a big risk: She moved a word from her reading vocabulary to her writing vocabulary, a word she had never before used in a piece of writing. That's what I mean by a language breakthrough.

In the Bronx, Denton, a first grader, wrote the story shown in Figure 3–1.

Where had Denton come upon *beloved,* an old-fashioned word that intermingles love, respect, and a kind of religious reverence? I told Denton: "It's a wonderful piece of writing. That word *beloved* makes it even more special to read."

I hoard yet one more vocabulary. This one has less to do with exotic words than with words saturated in strong memories. Words and phrases like *buffalo* and *mud puppy* contain potent medicine; their music conjures up an entire era of my life. I think of them as "trapdoor" words. For some words, the conventional meaning hides a secret trapdoor that leads down to an unexpected or previously forgotten layer of memory underneath. The mere mention of such a word is enough to bring it all back in a flood.

Take the word *sheriff.* This serious word has been altered forever by the association I have with Valerie Sheriff, a girl on whom I had a hopeless crush (the perfect word!) during eleventh and twelfth grades. She was stunning, and she was in the classes with all the smartest kids, which only intensified the awe in which I held her. Today I cannot watch a western with outlaws and sheriffs without immediately thinking of Valerie Sheriff, her straight blond hair and flawless features, the cool California air about her, the impossibly long legs beneath her cheerleader miniskirt, the energetic splits she did on the sidelines during football games that always left me feeling weak.

Or take *elegant.* My grandmother, Annie Collins, came from Arlington, Massachusetts, each year to spend Christmas with our family in New York. At our Christmas Eve dinner, Grandma Annie, Aunt Mary, my parents, and all seven or eight or nine kids would be sitting around the big table with the best plates and silverware, the food heaped high, a glass of red wine for the grownups, even a thimbleful for the kids. After the food was served, and grace said, everyone paused. We kids had to wait, drooling over our drumsticks, mouths watering over mounds of butternut squash with molten craters of butter on top. It was traditional that before the rest of us could dig in, Grandma Annie had to be the first one to take a mouthful of turkey.

"Oh, Jean, this is *elegant,*" she would say. That set everything into motion. Now Mom could blush her thanks, everyone else could laugh, and we could all start eating. But we knew. Young as we were, we understood

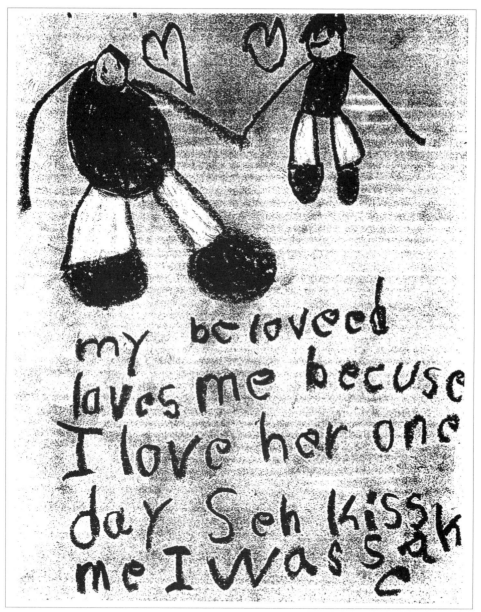

Figure 3-1

some of the significance of that word spoken here in New York by our Bostonian grandmother, a word that seemed to rhyme with "delicate," a word that carried its nostalgic ring of old Boston, maybe more civilized times, legends of Ted Williams and Jack Kennedy, the times she marched on the Boston Commons as a suffragette, and the night she danced with "Honey" Fitz at an office party in Filene's Bargain Basement, where she worked.

Grandma Annie died in 1979, at the age of ninety-two. Today, in my family, the word "elegant" still gets spoken around the holidays, and always with a great deal of reverence.

PART TWO

The Craft

FOUR
The Art of Specificity

Keep listening. Keep your radar out. Take everything, because it is matter for your work. No detail is too small.
MARY TALLMOUNTAIN

A FRIEND of mine broke up with his girlfriend. She seemed like a terrific person, bright and energetic. I asked him why.

"Lots of reasons," he said to me. "For one thing, she was eating too high off the food chain."

Ha! This remark—which still strikes me as hilarious—got carefully tucked away in my journal. I just knew that someday I would find a place for it in my writing: in a story, poem, or book.

A few years later I found myself teaching a college writing course. My students wrote with gusto; they wrote a great deal. If their writing had any generic weakness, it was the lack of specifics needed to substantiate points made in the text.

"You've got to get more specific," I said to the students during one class. "You're way too general. You can't expect readers to eat too high off the food chain."

Everyone laughed—myself included. But later, in a more sober moment, I decided that I actually liked the point I had made and even the way I had made it. In any piece of writing there is a kind of food chain, a continuum of thought ranging from the most general (nostalgia, Oedipal love, failed dreams) to the most concrete (burnt paper, a cat's sandpapery tongue, dead leaves scrape-dancing across sidewalk). Readers are omnivorous: they nourish themselves on the entire food chain. Still, each element on the chain depends on the element below it. Ultimately, as Donald Murray says, readers are "bottom feeders." The writing needs to be grounded in plenty of physical details. Without them the whole food chain falls apart.

As a boy I suffered from hay fever. Not just ragweed or goldenrod but also common grass right around mid-spring. When I rolled or wrestled in the grass my eyes would commence itching, whereupon I'd rub them, my hands now invisibly gloved in grass pollen. The itch would intensify. This prompted me to rub more vigorously still. Some afternoons would find my eyes nearly swollen shut.

Only my mother knew how to interrupt this cycle before I succeeded in tearing my eyes from their sockets. She'd bring me into the house, make me lie down, and put over my eyes a face cloth that had been soaked in cold water and folded to an inch and a half strip.

This helped. Pressed gently down, the wet cloth soothed those tortured orbs. And being deprived of my sight every day for forty-five minutes at a time taught me to pay attention to sounds and smells I had never before noticed. I heard my little brothers singing one of their silly songs outside the window:

> Mary, Mary, long before the fashions came,
> With her head chopped off and her belly, too,
> She looked so much like a moo . . .

Lying in darkness on the couch, I learned to distinguish whoever was coming down the stairs by the sounds of the footsteps. Not just Mom and Dad—that was easy—but also Jim or Elaine, Tom or Bob.

I listened to baseball. Only in total darkness could I fully picture those Red Sox games. Now the players came to life—not just their stats and quirks but also their exotic names. Pumpsie Green. Felix Mantilla. Bill Mombouquette. Some afternoons I would lie in blissful darkness and repeat that name—Bill Mombouquette (who was a great bunter for a pitcher, by the way)—fifty or sixty times.

And smells. The impossibly sweet spring air. The aroma of freshly mowed grass which entranced me even as it wreaked additional havoc on my allergies. The many different bodily odors soaked into the couch. A panoply of smoke smells I learned to differentiate: cigarette smoke (my mother), smoke from something frying on the stove (onions), and smoke from outside (someone in the neighborhood burning trash in their backyard incinerator).

BEAUTIFUL WRITING

Every writing teacher has at one time or another exhorted students: Get specific! I want to see concrete details! Pay closer attention to the particular! This suggests the irresistible argument for encouraging students to begin by writing from their own experience. Murray has pointed out that effective writing starts with "honest, specific, accurate" information. When students write from experience, they can breathe those specifics into their writing—

dialect, odd smells, precise names of plants—that can animate even the most tired and tedious text. The following narrative, by a fourth grader, begins with a distant, neutral tone as she lists her family's moves from town to town. But when the author slows down and goes under the surface, delving into the specifics, the effect is startling.

MY LIFE CHANGED
  When my parents got married they lived in the Bronx. Then they moved to Seaford. And that's when they had me. Three years later my parents had my sister. We were just moving out of Seaford. Then we moved to Merrick. And that's when something terrible happened. One year later when I was five and my sister was two, we were sleeping in my mom and dad's room. And then in the middle of the night, my dad got dressed, took some food and money, his briefcase for work, and just walked out. For some reason mom and dad always seemed to yell at each other. My only prayers and dreams are for them to get back together.

Those common household objects—food, money, briefcase—reverberate in my mind's eye and give a terrible concreteness to the father's departure.

I spent several days working with Dr. Linda Wells and a group of sixth-grade teachers in East Williston, New York. We were noticing that much of the student writing in those classes tended to be very literal, flat.

"When I talk about details with young writers," Linda Wells said, "I spend time talking about what a visual image is."

"It's funny," one teacher said, "because we've spent lots of time reading and rereading books with rich language, like *Owl Moon* (Jane Yolen). We read *I'm in Charge of Celebrations* (Byrd Baylor) and talked about the imagery. Those books are so beautiful, and the kids really loved them, but so far it hasn't had much effect on their writing."

"Wait a moment," I said. "Are we talking about *beautiful* writing or are we talking about *specific* writing?"

"That's just it," Linda said. She paused. "I've noticed that the writing becomes beautiful when it becomes specific, concrete."

The writing becomes beautiful when it becomes specific. That remark haunted me. I wrote it down. Thought about it. During the weeks that followed I began to suspect that Linda was right. In a sixth-grade class one boy wrote: "When I was a baby, I used to drag around this blanket. You couldn't pry it away from me. At night, I'd chew on the threads and they'd get caught in my teeth, like dental floss. My mother used to wait until I was asleep until she could reach into my mouth and try to pull out the threads."

The class laughed appreciatively. Another boy in the same class wrote: "When I was little, I used to take a silk scarf to bed with me. When my dad would kiss me goodnight, his eyebrow would brush the top of my forehead. I loved the way that felt. After he left and turned out the light, I'd take out the scarf. I found that if I rubbed the scarf with one hand, and my own eyebrow with the other, it would feel exactly like my father's eyebrow."

There is nothing exceptional in the words these writers use: blanket, dental floss, bushy eyebrows, silk. The power comes from the details and the absolute authority they lend to those early childhood memories, lovingly excavated and displayed before us. The writing becomes beautiful when it becomes specific.

I delighted in this poem by Lindsay, a third grader.

> *Eyes*
>
> Eyes are special things.
> They are slammed on your face
> when you are born.
> Eyes are what you see poems with
> and watch the world turn around and around.
>   If you did not have eyes
> you would not see your puppy slide across the porch
> when it's raining.

This writer knows how to see. In a single stroke she uses a few simple details, clearly observed, to create an ending of breathtaking clarity.

HOW SMALL DETAILS CAN EVOKE BIG ISSUES

In 1980 I wrote a feature article for *People* magazine about Dr. Joseph Panzarella, a quadriplegic doctor. Dr. Panzarella was the single most remarkable individual I ever met. Multiple sclerosis had left him without the use of his hands or legs. He needed an assistant to dress and feed him. A special hydraulic lift mounted on top of his car hoisted him to and from his wheelchair. Still, he managed to be medical director of a large rehabilitation hospital, the father of seven children, and author of a remarkable memoir, *Spirit Makes a Man.*

Panzarella and his wife, Josephine, were devoted to each other. But in the article I knew I didn't want to use that cliche: "devoted couple." I began looking for some example, some anecdote or detail from their life to illustrate the depth of their interconnectedness. One day Panzarella told me:

"Did you know that every night my wife wakes up every two hours and turns me in bed?" He smiled. "Otherwise I'd get bed sores. I can't turn myself. Can you imagine? Every two hours every night for the past fifteen years. She's some kind of woman."

I put that detail in my article.

A few years later I took a writing course from Richard Price. One afternoon during class Price leaned forward.

"The bigger the issue, the smaller you write," he said. "Remember that. You don't write about the horrors of war. No. You write about a kid's burnt socks lying on the road. There's this science fiction story where a guy comes back from space and finds that everyone on earth is dead from a nuclear war. He just drives around for a couple of days. But here's the thing: Even though he's the only one left, he still finds himself stopping for traffic signs, traffic lights. He can't help it. That's what you do. You pick the smallest manageable part of the big thing, and you work off the resonance."

The bigger the issue, the smaller you write. Very smart advice: possibly the single most important suggestion you will find in this book. It is the kind of insight that has taken me years to fully appreciate.

Recently I asked a high school teacher if there was a drug problem in his school. He smiled sadly, shook his head.

"Not really, not now, but let me tell you about something that happened a couple years ago. This kid got hurt one day on the athletic field. Broke his leg in three places. They had to bring in a helicopter and pull the kid out. The big copter—landed right on the field. When kids saw the helicopter, they panicked. 'The narcs are coming! The narcs are coming.' They rushed out of their classes and into the bathroom. All you could hear was the sound of toilets flushing and flushing all over the school."

The story in Figure 4–1 was written by Katie, a first grader whose mother had died two years earlier. Nearly every piece of writing she completed that year had something to do with this tragic event.

The bigger the issue, the smaller you write. You don't write about a serious drug problem. You write about a helicopter landing and the sound of toilets flushing frantically throughout a high school. You don't write about the death of a mother: You write about how "her voice got quieter."

The writers whose work is cited in this chapter are not afraid to let their readers get close to the raw materials of their stories. They trust that, given enough specifics, enough information, the reader is wholly capable of making the leap from the concrete to the larger issue.

Concrete details allow the writer to *understate* an important truth rather than clubbing the reader over the head with it. Such details have an almost

From Katie to Mom
I Love you mom and I no
you do to and owes will to
and I do to mom   my mom lick
to sing and wen hr vos got
quitr I seing for hr
She lick to clect cauot Things
and I gave hr ston acotsm

bat mom
can stil
hir me.

my mom is
sing in The
picks ra.

Figure 4-1

I love you mom and I know you do too and always will, too. And I do too, mom.
My mom liked to sing and when her voice got quieter I sang for her. She liked to
collect cute things. And I gave her (grave) stone a cute snowman. But mom can
still hear me. My mom is singing in the picture.

magical way of getting to the heart of complex issues, making explanations unnecessary.

THE RECURRING DETAIL

Freud pointed out that as human beings we hunger for recurrent experience. This helps to explain both the cyclical nature of mythology and a fundamental element of story: The details mentioned early in the story usually recur, often with more significance, toward the end of the story. No accident that Cinderella lost a slipper while running from the ball. No coincidence that Piggy's glasses are used to start a fire early in *Lord of the Flies*. These details help set up the events that will follow.

"If in the first chapter you say that a gun hung on the wall," Chekhov said, "in the second or third chapter it must without fail be discharged."

In Aliki's *The Two of Them*, the grandfather makes a ring for his grand-daughter on the day of her birth. The girl grows up, spending long stretches of time with her grandfather. The ring makes a few sly appearances in the book's lovely illustrations but does not get mentioned in the text until a crucial moment in the book:

> Time passed,
> and the ring fit the little girl's finger,
> and it seemed, suddenly,
> that grandfather was an old man.
> One night he became ill,
> and after that,
> part of him could not move.

In Aliki's book, the ring would seem to work on many levels: keepsake, sign of the girl's maturity, symbol suggesting the circularity of life.

Many young writers have a difficult time juggling the details in their writing. Frank, a second grader, wrote:

> A boy went into the forest. He found a frog and put it into his pocket. He kept walking and found an old house. An old man lived there. He invited the boy into the house for lunch. "Okay," said the boy.

The story continued for many pages. It turned out, of course, that the old man was a dangerous wizard out to capture the little boy for his wicked purposes. I had a writing conference with Frank.

"What I'm wondering is, what happened to the frog?" I asked. "I kept expecting to hear about that frog in the boy's pocket."

Frank looked surprised.

"Oh, there's no more about the frog," he explained, shrugging. "That was just the beginning of the story." He was utterly unaware of the expectation he had raised in this reader.

A detail mentioned early that shows up later can provide a deeply satisfying resolution to any piece of writing. Genevieve, a fourth grader, wrote this story:

THE SAD DAYS

When I was four years old I used to have a blanket I would carry around. But one Sunday morning I woke up and it wasn't there. I asked my mom where Mr. Blanky was and she said: "It's in the attic." I said: "Why is it in the attic?" and she said: "You are growing up now. You're not supposed to carry a blanket around." So I went to my room and cried.

On my birthday when I turned five years old my mommy gave me a teddy bear. I was so happy then I started holding that all the time. But one day my father was so mad he stole it away from me because every time I started walking with it I would knock things down. He put it in the attic with Mr. Blanky.

One rainy afternoon my mom started screaming and I was scared but then my father called Grandma to stay with us while Mommy and Daddy went to the hospital. A couple of days later she came back crying and I asked her why she was crying and she said: "I lost the baby." I said: "What?" She said she had a miscarriage but I didn't understand.

When I was seven years old I asked her again and she explained it to me. Then I went upstairs in the attic, took down Mr. Blanky, and gave it to my mom to make her feel better because Mr. Blanky always made me feel better every time I was sad.

The recurring detail works like an echo in which the second mention is nearly always more important than the first. In the following poem of mine, a jug of cider gets hidden in a river at the beginning of the poem. The jug of cider recurs at the end of the poem, transformed into something larger than itself.

River Heart

Close to the moist bank of the creek
my brother and I enter the forest.
We hide a jug of fresh apple cider,
wedged underwater between mossy stones,
and follow the stream up forest.

Later it gets hot and we branch off
through a stand of stunted pines
with bear tracks and deer droppings.

Everything here is dark and still.
We sit down to share our only apple.
"We're lost," my little brother sighs
and tries mightily not to cry.
The trees have veins like Mom's legs,
hiding us under huge hushed skirts.
Tons of raw pine creak above us.
The wind dies and Bobby jumps up:
"I hear the river calling to us!"

Off he goes and finds the creek!
It curves and hisses and glistens,
a silver snake caressed by the sun.
We race downstream to the wet place
where the cider alone awaits our return.
I lift it out, dripping, triumphant,
an icy throbbing river heart.

We drink it slowly
walking home
and I feel the river's pulse
in my bones.

FIVE
Creating a Character

A writer should know how much change a character has in his pockets.
JAMES JOYCE

I RECENTLY CONDUCTED an intense poetry seminar with two dozen teachers and administrators in Burlington, Massachusetts. We spent an hour writing poems of our own. Just before lunch I asked if anyone would like to read aloud what they had written. Awkward pause. Carla Panciera, a young teacher I had just met that day, tentatively raised her hand.

"It's not quite done," she said, "but I'll read it."

One Piece of my Father

A "v" revealed through the neck
of his cotton shirt, a triangle
two fingers spread could frame,
perfect, brown as his face,
the disturbed earth, my eyes
that are, instead, my mother's.
The corner of him that knows
the sun up close
from high on a tractor
pacing the horizon, or
from a barn he shingles
with the cedar he cut months ago
when the swamp was frozen,
or looking up the way he did
to judge a piece of sky:
sun for hay, rain for corn,
clouds for relief, a small space
of man, a glimpse of work,
a spot to rest against, up close
to ask a question to
to force him to look down.

When she finished reading there was a long pause. Sensing that no one else would dare follow that poem, I said: "Well, I guess it's time for lunch."

A story requires the intersection of three spheres:

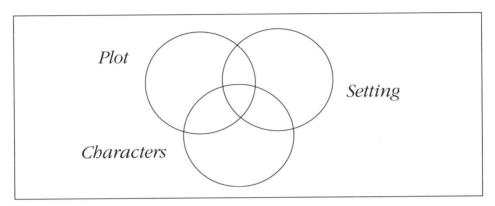

Innumerable links, large and infinitesimal, connect these three elements. Character drives plot (Ahab is obsessed with killing the white whale), which gets sculpted by the setting (the man makes one last attempt to build the fire, but it is seventy-five degrees below zero and by now his hands have grown numb), which, in its turn, is affected by the characters in the story (the soldiers set fire to the plantation).

But character remains preeminent. The characters contain the crucial human link, that element of human destiny, for the reader to identify with.

Writers will forever wrestle with the challenge of creating characters that get up off the page and step into our lives. The great writers use a few deft strokes or odd details to create characters with an apparent effortlessness that takes our breath away. Suddenly, we feel we have known them our entire lives: Buck or Charlotte, Randall McMurphy or Scarlett O'Hara.

When I am trying to create a character, either a real or imagined person, I try for a healthy balance between the public and private persona:

PUBLIC	*PRIVATE*
Accomplishments	Emotions
Biographical background	Quirks
Appearance	Inner strengths and fears

Whether describing historical figures (presidents, baseball players, explorers, inventors) or fictional characters (human beings or animals), young writers need help in breathing life into their characters. These writers typically find it easier to describe a character's public persona than to bring forth what the reader really wants: a sense of the character's inner being.

THE PHYSICAL BEING

"After World War Two I used to go to a lot of dances," Bill Gregory, a third-grade teacher, told me. "I could always tell which of the young women had been working in a factory during the war. It wasn't just their skin, which was too white. It wasn't just that pinched look around their eyes. It was their hands. The factory girls were the ones who always had callouses on their palms."

Our bodies are maps that tell the stories of our lives: triumphs, scars, stamina, the inroads of death. When writers explore the terrain of the physical, we help readers enter more fully into the life of our characters. Here is a fine opportunity for writers to use their most important tools—the five senses.

Touch: "When Grandpa kissed me goodnight his stubbly cheek felt like a piece of old sandpaper from the garage."

Sound: "In the morning, I listened to my mother trying to clear her lungs. Some days she'd hack away for a half hour or forty minutes. She had two distinct kinds of coughs. The wet one sounded like each lung was snarled in long wet strips of cloth. The dry cough sounded like the last few nails being pounded into a block of wood, or a coffin . . ."

Sight: "She had long arms and bony elbows. When she cut her meat, she reminded me of one of those big sea birds trying to gain altitude . . ."

Smell: "She worked in a candy store, and the smell of fudge was soaked into her; my mouth watered whenever she gave me a hug."

When students write about someone familiar as a mother or close friend, they often have a too deeply internalized sense of the person or pet to describe the character with real objectivity. Such writers may not realize that the words on the page do not provide enough information for the reader to form a clear image of the character. In such cases, the writing teacher might ask the student to literally "flesh out" the character by using the five senses.

I talked with Meredith, a second grader who had just written the first draft of the following poem:

> *Grand Parents*
>
> My grandpa is still alive . . .
> My grandma is dead ohh poo!
> Oh, why did you die?

"It's not very good," Meredith said. "It's so short."

"Is the poem about your grandmother or your grandfather?" I asked her.

"My grandmother, really."

"Your grandmother. All right, how about if you just concentrate on her?"

"All right."

"Help me picture her."

"Well, she had a really big warm smile," Meredith said. "She had curly gold hair . . ."

A few minutes later, Meredith had tried a slightly more expansive draft of her poem:

> she is beautiful
> she has a warm smile
> she has brown eyes
> she also has curly hair
> that's my grandma

When Meredith and I talked some more, I encouraged her to teach me everything she knew about her grandmother. Her final draft showed little resemblance to what she started with.

> *Special Ending*
>
> She's beautiful
> Warm smile
> Brown eyes
> Curly gold hair
>
> Lived near me
> Went to parks
> Sailed boats
>
> Now she's dead
> Left behind for me
> Golden earrings
> They mean the world to me.

THE TELLING DETAIL

Deft characterization can be slow, painstaking work. But it doesn't have to be laborious. Sometimes a writer can bring a character to life with a single, carefully chosen detail. There is an art to this, of course; find the right specific and every aspect of the character comes into instant focus for the reader, right down to the color of his socks, her earrings.

I know a woman, a phenomenal cook. Cream of carrot soup that would make you weep. If you ask for the recipe, she'll give it to you, carefully typed, with an obliging smile. Unfortunately, she has already subtly altered the ingredients. No matter how hard you try, no matter how painstakingly you follow her recipe, your soup will never approach hers.

His mother fed him four slices of white bread before dinner so he would not eat too much meat.

The boy rode on his brand new bicycle, down the driveway, onto the sidewalk and—crash! He fell forward, right onto his face. He lay there motionless. The bike continued a few feet further before it, too, slammed into the pavement, the front wheel still spinning. With a cry his mother rushed down the driveway, past her son, and bent to examine the bicycle.

In a gangster novel, the author introduced a dangerous young man: "He was a well-dressed young man, and he wore cufflinks reputedly made from human bone."

In *Miss Maggie*, a picture book by Cynthia Rylant, Nat, a boy, develops a friendship with Miss Maggie, an old Appalachian woman.
> Sometimes Miss Maggie rode to the grocery store with Nat and his grandfather. Nat would wait in the truck when Miss Maggie went into the store, because she always had a wad of tobacco in her jaw and she'd spit it just anywhere she pleased. Nat was afraid people might think she was a relative.

That single detail—spitting tobacco juice inside a store—goes a long way toward convincing the reader that this woman is an outsider who has never wholly adapted herself to mainstream society.

The revelatory detail can also act as a dramatic clue to show a character undergoing a crucial metamorphosis.

> George's grandfather was a formal and fastidious dresser. Even on a summer day of eighty degrees, he would come downstairs wearing a clean white shirt, tie, light jacket, with every hair in place.
> One day, during a visit with his grandfather, George noticed that the old man was as impeccably dressed as usual except for one thing: the belt was outside one of the loops in his pants. George didn't say anything. But two mornings later, he noticed his grandfather's belt had missed two loops on one side, and one loop on the other.

The bigger the issue, the smaller you write. Don't write about senility or a man losing the ability to take care of himself. Write about missed belt loops. Put forth the raw evidence, and trust that the reader will understand exactly what you are getting at.

SPOKEN WORDS

Peter is a smoker, in his fifties somewhere, with deep lines on his face. A face with character: suffering. When I met Peter, my first reaction was that his face had melted and slipped about two inches. Catholic school background. My overall impression is that he should have retired a long time ago. The man is nasty to his ninth-grade students, even with me sitting there in the classroom.

"Look at that," he barks at one student. "Hey, what, can you read that? Do you include a magnifying glass with your story? Write larger!"

His students are silent as he moves around the room.

"Michael, I'm confused about something. Are *you* the teacher? Oh, I see. *I* am. So hey, when I say you need to change your conclusion, I mean *change* it. *Improve* it."

At one point Peter loudly crumples up one girl's story and throws it into the grey wastepaper basket. Still glaring at the girl, he rushes to the front of the room and grabs a piece of chalk.

"A map!" he shouts. "M-A-P. The assignment was to map out your story *before* you write. What, hey, am I speaking Swahili here or what?"

Peter quickly sketches a map of New York with Long Island, a horizontal fish, at the bottom.

"Here's Nassau County," he says, marking it with an X. "Here's Albany. How do I get there?"

One boy cautiously raises his hand; Peter jabs a finger at him.

"Drive?"

"All right, you can drive!" Peter roars back. "Fine! Is there just one way of getting there?"

No?

"No!" He's on a roll now; he speaks in rapid rhythm. "You can take the Taconic State Parkway. You can take the New York State Thruway. You can go over to Jersey and take Route 17 north. There's all kinds of ways to go. How do you know which one to use?"

"Look at a map . . . ?" one boy suggests.

"Right!" Peter is nearly beside himself. "You look at a map to plan your route! What do—look, I don't care which way you go, but I want to know that *you* know which way you're going. Make a map first! That's what I've been trying to tell you! My point is—and follow the map when you write! And if you start writing something that's *not* on the map—what? What?"

Pause. The students stare at him.
Peter screams: "You're *on the wrong road!*"

We reveal ourselves by what we say, how we say it, what we do not say. A writer develops an ear for dialogue by learning how to eavesdrop: listening to the spoken word.

John Burningham's picture book *Granpa* contains a series of moments between a girl and her grandfather. The book is written almost entirely in simple dialogue, without speaker tags, so the reader is invited to figure out just who says what. My favorite page reads:

"When we get to the beach can we stay there forever?"
"Yes, but we must come home for our tea at four o'clock."

Even the youngest writer can see that the word "forever" is a potent clue, that the words of the first sentence were spoken by the child.

Written dialogue, when it sounds authentic, is filled with the grammatical errors, sentence fragments, interruptions, grunts, sighs, and spontaneous wit that make human speech what it is. It is important to learn to listen not to what a person is trying to say but what that person actually says.

Andrew is an extraordinarily gifted second grader from Mt. Prospect, Illinois. One morning he had a peer conference with a girl in the class.

"What are you writing about today?" he asks.

"I think I'm going to write about my dog who died."

"That's the spirit!" Andrew says cheerfully. The boy laughs, glances at the teacher. "Get it, Mrs. Weiss? The dog died! *That's the spirit!*"

Later that day, Janet Weiss puts the kids through a basic math review. Andrew groans.

"Aw Mrs. Weiss, if I'd known that this was all I was going to learn today I would've stayed on the bus."

Spoken dialogue has the uncanny ability to conjure up an entire world. I collect in my journal stray bits of dialogue, snatches of conversation that evoke a mood or a bigger, though unspoken, issue. One morning, while walking in the park, I came upon a couple, around thirty, arguing on a bench.

"I'm tired of riding the rollercoaster of your moods," the woman hissed in a whisper. "I want to get off!"

In a first-grade classroom, a girl has just read her cat story to the class. When she finishes a boy raises his hand.

"You need to keep your cat in a cage," he says.

"No, we don't do that," she replies.

"Well, the cat'll scratch up the furniture."

"We don't have a cage. My mother puts patches on the furniture."

"Wow," the boy says. "Your mom is nice!"

"She is nice," the girl replies. Pause. "To cats."

"I wish I were a cat," the boy is saying. "I'd go live with your mom."

GESTURE AND MOTION

Taylor is never so content as when he's sitting next to his mother, the two fingers of his right hand stuck in his mouth, the fingers of the other hand playing with JoAnn's exuberant hair. He plays with it idly, glancing up now and then at the dark mass, then down, twirling it tight, letting it come loose, a motion that reminds me of nothing so much as the cotton candy makers at the fair, wrapping sugary webs around the thin white paper cones.

At 6:30 A.M. Adam makes his first down payment on breakfast: a bowl of Golden Graham cereal and orange juice. He gulps it down quickly. In between bites, he races from the table to his spot in front of the television, a ring of milk around his mouth, then back again when his mouth is empty. Later, when JoAnn and I have breakfast, Adam is there for his second installment, whatever we are having: pancakes, oatmeal, scrambled eggs, muffins. He is fully capable of three such breakfasts before he finally quits, secure in the knowledge that lunch is never too far off.

The kids who are best at playing war are the kids who know how to die the best. Every kid knows this. This was true when I was young, and I would be surprised if it were not equally true today. When I played war nobody could die more fiercely, more convincingly, than my old friend Freddy Fletcher (no relation). His deaths had a life of their own: the sudden slack-jawed clutch at his wounded torso, the long, drawn-out virulent howl, the sound of a final breath being ripped from his lungs. His frame had a strange way of hanging there, twisting, for a few seconds. Then his body went board-rigid, already a victim of rigor mortis, a moment before he hurtled forward and down onto the hard ground. "He's dead, all right," I'd mutter to myself, even as I marveled how he had managed to avoid mashing his nose on the ground.

Get your characters moving. Old saying: You can tell more about a man by the way he cuts his meat than by anything else. Two boys go into the forest for a picnic. One boy has brought some juice, potato chips, and two apples. The other boy has brought a whole small cooked chicken. When they begin eating, the first boy rips off an entire chicken leg and begins gnawing hungrily. The other boy wrinkles his nose, takes out a gleaming knife, cuts off a single slice of white meat from the very top of the chicken, and places it carefully on a napkin. He takes out a fork and begins to eat.

Gestures can clearly reveal a character's emotional or physical state, as in this tender poem by Michelle, a second grader:

> *Only with Him*
>
> Only with him
> I love to stay.
> He is very busy
> but he could find
> some time to stay
> with me.
> I love going to the
> movies with him
> where it's dark.
> Even though he
> falls asleep.
> I still love my father.

THE FLASH-DRAFT

> Soft feet pound the ground. A sleek, shiny body pounces on a young deer. Strong claws break the deer's neck. The cougar, Ghost of the Rockies, has made its kill.
> Strictly carnivorous, the cougar's chief prey are deer and elk. . . .

JoAnn Curtis first conceived of the flash-draft as a way to help students internalize and communicate information in content-area writing. The student begins by creating a specific character and by putting that character into a brief scene, anecdote, or story. The flash-draft might never become part of the final report. But by having the student focus on one specific character at one particular moment, the flash-draft gives students a narrative vehicle for bringing alive that character and the larger world in which that character lives.

One group of third graders wrote flash-drafts for the animals they were studying.

> One morning when the panda woke up, his zoo keeper was right outside his cage with an apple for breakfast. On the other side of the world the panda's brother is laying down on the grass chewing the bamboo leaves.
> *Scott S.*

Lindsey brought her animal alive using a comparison between the animal's life and her own life:

> When I'm getting ready for bed the panther wakes up from its sleep and goes hunting for its prey. Then, so no animal can touch the panther's food, it goes up to the top of the tree carrying its prey and comes back with more food for her cubs.

I was sufficiently impressed by the voice and energy in these third graders' writing that I decided to try the flash-draft with a group of fifth-grade students who had been studying South American cultures.

"Put your notes away," I said to the students. "I want you to think of a character, and see if you can put that character into a story. You might pick a famous character or an ordinary person. Make it as true, as authentic, as you possibly can. You might try to use what you've learned about weather or geography in your flash-draft."

Jessica Abrams wrote about a poor mountain girl:

> Waneta woke up at five o'clock in the morning. As she walks outside, she sees how high up she is. Waneta lives in Lima, Peru. She is poor. Her family grows food such as cabbages. It is very hard to grow food in the poor soil of the Andes mountains. Waneta is ten years old. She sits down and braids her hair with one, long, shiny black braid. It is a tradition in her town for everybody to wear a braid. . . .

Jessica's flash-draft has much to commend it: a sense of place, an attention to the particular. But for me, at least, it works primarily because I believe in the character of Waneta, who springs to life in my imagination through that "one, long, shiny black braid."

I suggested the flash-draft to an eighth-grade English class that had been studying topics related to the Great Depression. The flash-drafts were written during class time and entirely without notes; the best of them showed a skillful interweaving of information and narrative, with a single character at the center.

WALT DISNEY

> Amy gripped the armrest of the chair with her hands. Her palms were sweaty with excitement. Finally, her mother had taken her to see the new film: "Snow White and the Seven Dwarfs." Amy remembered when Walt Disney had first created Mickey Mouse. Now he was her hero. The lights dimmed: the show was about to begin.
>
> Walt Disney, a hero of children of all ages, was called the "master of make-believe." He, like many others, was brought down by the Depression in the early 30's. Disney made many cartoons including "The Three Little Pigs."

The song "Who's Afraid of the Big Bad Wolf" referred to the big bad social wolf . . . the Depression. Disney's song became very popular, and was played almost as often as the other songs of the ages.

In 1935 Walt Disney won a medal for Mickey Mouse calling him a "symbol of international good will." Disney's cheery characters helped many people through tough times.

As Amy left the movie theatre she felt very happy. Things were hard at home, but she felt good knowing that at the movies there would always be a happy ending.

SIX
Voice

Writing with voice is writing into which someone has breathed. It has that fluency, rhythm, and liveliness that exist naturally in the speech of most people when they are enjoying a conversation.... Writing with real voice *has the power to make you pay attention and understand—the words go deep.*
PETER ELBOW, *Writing with Power*

THE FOLLOWING COMPOSITION was written by an eighth-grade boy:

THE COMPOSITION

Boy, this burns me up. I look around the room, and everyone is writing except for me. There is only one thing flashing through my mind. "What should I write about?" I always feel there is a black hole inside of me regarding a topic.

I always get hot under the collar when my English teacher asks what we are up to in our compositions. Everyone says, "Second draft" or "Finished." I usually say: "First draft" and everyone around me gives me the evil eye. I try to remember experiences in my life that I could write about but nothing comes to mind. And even if I get an idea on paper, it never works out the way I want.

Every teacher says don't worry about the grammar, punctuation, and spelling until you edit your work; just get something down on your paper. I worry about the grammar even before I write a piece, which confuses me. With every piece I write, there is always something telling me that people are not going to like it. This ruins my train of thought.

Then there is a problem I have expressing my thoughts. I can tell someone a story but can't describe it on a piece of paper. When I write a piece I am proud of, it usually receives a bad grade, but when write a piece I don't like, it usually receives a fairly good grade.

One of the two things that distresses me most is when I see people whose pieces are two or three pages long. Then I look at my composition, and it is only one page long. This makes me believe that the people with bigger compositions are going to get a better grade because their composition is longer than mine. Some kids in class come up to me and ask if the teacher accepts my one page composition.

"Yes, he does." For this reason alone I am going to end this piece here.

The last chapter explored ways of creating character. But the one character writers most consistently fail to develop is the narrator. Too often the narrator (or main character) becomes little more than observer, a neutral teller-of-tales about whose inner life we learn little.

Writing of this kind lacks voice.

People get confused about *voice*. What is it? Style? Tone? Is it always informal?

When I talk about voice, I mean written words that carry with them the sense that someone has actually written them. Not a committee, not a computer: a single human being. Writing with voice has the same quirky cadence that makes human speech so impossible to resist listening to. Dark humor, numerous cryptic asides, and a terrific ending make "The Composition" such a pleasure to read. The author creates an ironic tension between his topic (an inability to write well) and the composition itself, which is written with real authority. This writing has energy: juice.

Many people who are charming in person find it difficult to sound natural, to sound like themselves, on the page. Developing voice in one's writing requires awareness and diligence; it probably also requires a patient, supportive mentor or writing teacher. Those of us who work with young writers might consider a two-stage approach for encouraging students to develop voice: helping them explore their "inner writing voice," and showing them ways of keeping some of that voice intact when the writing goes public, goes formal.

STALKING YOUR INNER VOICE

While working on this book, I discovered that writing really does have a kind of symmetry. A balancing act. Tension and resolution. Dramatic scene and narrative summary. Action and reflection. A beginning that fits with the ending.

Likewise, the writer balances the characters' external and internal lives. And one way of revealing the internal life of the narrator or other character is through the inner voice.

Everyone has an inner voice. But the writer is different from everyone else; the writer listens. She pays attention to it. Frequently she will drop everything to write down whatever it has to say. If the inner voice gets skittish at her approach, she tries sneaking up to it. Coos soothingly. Tries tossing out a few crumbs. The writer may not know exactly what the inner voice represents (unconscious? superego? spirit?) but the writer does know one thing: the inner voice is spokesperson for the inner life.

In Annie Dillard's *Pilgrim at Tinker Creek,* there is a marvelous essay on stalking the misunderstood muskrat. Toward the end the author asserts: "You have to stalk the spirit, too."

The writer must learn how to stalk the inner voice. At least I find I must. It whispers to me continuously, all year, but the pace of my life makes it difficult to tune in. To tune inward. And when I finally get around to doing so, all too often the inner voice bolts. Vanishes.

I use a journal to stalk my inner voice. (I know it has become fashionable to refer to it as a writer's notebook instead of a journal, but I still fussily insist on referring to mine as a journal.) The arena of my journal is where I spend a lot of time trying to write comfortably, chatting on paper, chumming up to my—what? Consciousness? Mind's eye? I don't really know what to call it, though it is probably the central tool I have as a writer.

July 8, 1990. In this journal I will try to slow down. The farmhouse in East Wells, Vermont. A much needed week in the country. A much neater trick, of course, would be to slow down at home in Paramus, New Jersey, at the frenetic intersection of Route 17 and Route 4. Still, you have to start somewhere.

Slow down. Give each thought its due, its space. For example: I have discovered that I like writing on the right side of my journal better than the left. The pages lie flatter.

Up early, play with Robert while JoAnn sleeps, bring him back upstairs for a second round of nursing. Back downstairs, I immediately set to stalking (I once wrote "wire-tapping") my inner voice. 7:30 A.M. Eerie quiet outside. The deck is moist with dew. The trickle from the brook. I walk with bare feet over wet grass to the far edge of the lawn. Looking back at the house, I see a large skunk sauntering across the wooden bridge of the creek. Sauntering like he owns the place. Which I suppose he does.

Thoreau once wrote an essay where he talked about the word *saunter.* He was talking about walking, a leisurely kind of walking and reflecting on life. Saunter, Thoreau suggested, might have been derived from the French words *sans* and *terre* ("without the earth"). When you saunter, you are not rooted to your path, to the physical earth. Rather, you can let your thoughts wander.

That seems like the perfect word for this kind of journal. Time enough (and room enough) to saunter.

I come back to the house, make coffee, bring it outside to the table I'm writing on. I read a magazine. The tall flower—larkspur?—growing at the edge of the deck is the most vivid purple I have ever seen. The purple challenges me: C'mon, write something good. Poetic.

I'm stalking, all right, but I can tell it will be a slow approach. Having trouble locking in the proper frequency. Dillard names the old classic rule about stalking: "Stop often 'n set frequent." I am stopping. I am setting. Trying to be patient.

First, this stray bit of consciousness to attend to—strange, true, nearly forgotten in the grinding rush to finish up work. For the past ten days or so I have stumbled out of bed in the morning with the name Cory McFlintock in my mind. She—only her name (*Is* Cory always a girl's name?)—appears most distinctly when I stagger into the bathroom, take off my pj's, and start my shower.

I have no explanation for this. Maybe I heard the name somewhere (the radio?) and it got buried in my memory. Still, why should it persist for two weeks in coloring the beginnings of each day?

Who are you, Cory McFlintock? What do you want from me?

Tomorrow I will take this chair and place it on the wooden bridge. Let the tumbling waters below whisper encouragement to my inner voice: flow, words. Flow, memory.

It's painful getting back in touch with my inner voice. It forces me to ask big grown-up questions about my life. When a person has been tied up for several hours, the first sensation you get when you are untied is one of excruciating pain as the blood flows back and remembers(!) the areas that have been cut off from circulation. Bring a frostbitten person into a warm house, he or she will be fine until the frozen extremities start thawing out. Then cover your ears.

My inner voice, long ignored, finally attended to, responds by howling bitterly. Where the hell have *you* been? Do you think you can snap me on and off like a radio? Take a good look at yourself. You are a writer, a poet. When you ignore me, you ignore yourself.

I have no suitable response save to write it all down. Just possibly Cynthia Rylant and Jane Yolen were right when they suggested, in separate interviews with me, the notion of some higher power that writes *through* them. Why not? I'm willing to believe in the magic. I'm going to put a piece of apple pie and a carrot right by the fireplace, right beneath the hung stockings. When static obscures the inner voice, when the tracks get faint, I will read, breathe, talk a walk, dream, play with my son. Wait and see what happens.

Wait. Franz Kafka had the motto—*Warte*—written on the wall above his bed. Sounds easy. Who has time for waiting?

(Later, the inner voice started flowing, not when I expected, while I was ready, journal open, pen in hand, but while I was playing with Robert and studying his two-month-old head. Not in complete sentences, either. In fragments. Words.)

Newspapers trumpeting global warming. Global thawing between U.S. and Soviets. Emerging global economy. The globe of Robert's little head. JoAnn: "Don't you just love the changing topography of his face?" On top his head is like the Arctic circle: tundra, not much growing up there. Wide expanses of skull, scalp, thinly growing hair. The soft spot: fontanel. Etymology of that word? Check. Expandable skull for a mushrooming brain. Fontanel. From above, looks exactly like adult-sized lips. Like something dark has bent down to put its kiss, the imprint of its lips, on Robert's head. Makes me hold him more tightly.

His hair: fine, brown, a hint of red under certain light. JoAnn's father laughed, never seen an Italian baby with reddish hair. Thin as my own hair. Already an endangered species.

Eyebrows (barely visible) forming a line along the globe's equator. Major facial features (eyes, ears, nose, mouth) all scrunched down below this equator.

His eyes are surprisingly, exuberantly blue. Temporary? They will fade to brown, we think, though we are prepared to be surprised. Eyes alert, expressive, cross-eyed at times. Heavy and swollen after he nurses. Eyeballs soaked in milk.

(Sometimes the inner voice doesn't whisper—it screams.)

Four months later. Robert six months old. At the supermarket people stare and lavish attention on Robert. "What a little doll," one lady said. To her seven-year-old: "Wouldn't you love to find *that* under the Christmas tree on Christmas morning?"

I smiled tensely, made my exit, but my inner voice was beserk: "Look, lady, he's *not* some little doll. He's a complex little human, a Homo sapien seething with instinct, emotion, song, story, archetype, language. Get back! Don't you dare put a bow on my son!"

Then again, maybe fatherhood has made me a little high-strung.

One use of a journal or notebook is to jumpstart the mind. But another purpose, equally important, is to provide a place to relax, to settle into a comfortable writing stride. I try to let some of that easy journal voice leak into the writing I do for publication. It is an indirect process. I think of my readers as one person. I figure that if that person can get a sense of me as a person he might, in turn, listen to what I have to say.

Helping young writers find this inner voice starts with time—giving young writers the regular time they need. A five-minute "journal write" first thing each morning, while the teacher takes lunch count, probably isn't enough. They need sustained time.

"Too often in classrooms we give children little squirts of language," Bill Martin says. "We squirt at them, and they squirt back."

We can also teach students to revise for voice. Read it back. Listen to how the writing sounds. Which parts sound most like you? Are there places where you can hear yourself chatting to a friend? Do certain parts sound stiff and awkwardly formal? Listen for real voice in these two sentences: "We rode rapidly to the store" or "We raced to the store."

Voice is connected to real audience. We have to create classrooms where writers have a wide, sympathetic audience for their writing. We need to encourage students to meet their audience in authentic ways—not just by sharing sessions with their peers but also by going public with their writing in other ways beyond the walls of the classroom: complaint letters, articles, contests, etc.

FINDING A WRITING VOICE

Suzanne Gardinier, poet and colleague of mine, says that voice in writing has much to do with an *intimacy* between writer and subject: a close distance between the author and what is being written about. In voiceless writing, the author stands far back from the subject. Such distance can impart a cold, detached feel to the writing. When writing has real voice, you can sense the author pulling in close, cozying up to the subject, as in the poem by Danielle, a first-grade writer (see Figure 6–1).

"Ho I sey." I love that boldness, the utter lack of artifice. I can just picture this first grader beaming as she announces her wonder to the world. The following piece was written by Theresa, also a first grader:

MY HUNNYBUN

After my Hunnybun tacks us to school my Hunnybun gos to work. My Hunnybun works in the kichin in the school. My Hunnybun gives the kids thar hot lunch but some of the kids give Hunnybun a hard time. After work my Hunnybun picks us up from school. then we go home or shopping or she take me to danceschool. and ges how my Hunnybun is = my mommy.

The inevitability of Theresa's ending does not detract from this charming and tender portrait of a mother. These pieces of writing are not atypical; it's not uncommon to find young children writing with voice. For older students, however, writing with real voice becomes more the exception than

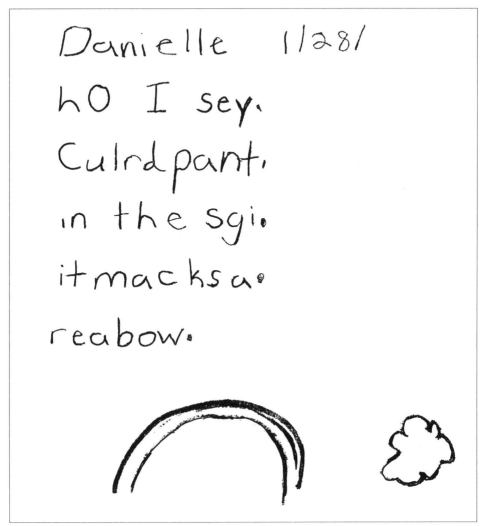

Danielle 1/28/

hO I sey.

Culrd pant.

in the sgi.

it macks a.

reabow.

Figure 6-1

the rule. I have worked in many upper-grade classrooms populated by writers who have lost their voice.

What kills it? I'd finger *audience* as the major murder suspect. As students get older, the audience for their writing undergoes a shift. As they approach adolescence, they tend to become more self-critical, particularly in terms of writing. This internal shift gets reinforced by tougher demands from the outside world. The supportive writing environment in the primary grades, often flavored with a child-centered or developmental philosophy about learning, yields to upper-grade realities of grading, book reports, grammar dittoes, writing tests, the five-paragraph essay, etc.

Voice is one area where older writers can learn from younger ones. Often, the work of young writers contains an intimacy not just between the writer and subject but also between writer and audience. Young writers regularly demonstrate an uncanny ability to reach out from the page, to converse freely with the reader. This story was written by a second grader:

> Hi these are my frends. see my perins are divores. it isn't fun having perins ho ar divres't ao I omost frgot My name is Lauren. at frest youl do a lot of crying. but you'l get uest to it. you now it didin't tarn awt so bad see. but after a long time don't think you are the one ho made the divores becas It wasin't it was bitwene your perens so i tink divors is fun in a way so see evn thowe your perins are divors it still is fun living withaut your Mom ore dad by the way tangnks for lisining!

> Hi. These are my friends. See, my parents are divorced. It isn't fun having parents who are divorced. Oh, I almost forgot, my name is Lauren. At first you'll do a lot of crying. But you'll get used to it. You know, it didn't turn out so bad, see? But after a long time don't think you are the one who made the divorce because it wasn't, it was between your parents. So I think divorce is fun in a way. So even though your parents are divorced it still is fun living without your Mom or Dad. By the way, thanks for listening!

It is rarer to see a story with voice from an older student. This story was written by Gina Pedone, a twelve-year-old writer from Merrick, New York. It is the searching honesty of this narrative that makes the voice sound so authentic.

> When my brother was born, he wasn't exactly a bouncing baby boy. He had a lot of problems with his insides, and well I just couldn't understand it then. I was still waiting for my teeth to come out for the tooth fairy.

> A lot of times mom would stay at the hospital helping the nurse care for the sick child. Back then I didn't know what was happening and I got jealous. He got cared for 24 hours a day and I got stuck with next-door neighbors who tried feeding me orange marmalade sandwiches.

> After five operations the doctors said he was well enough to come home. Just to look at him would bring tears to your eyes. He was always pale and had to be fed through a tube from inside his stomach. A lot of times he would pull out the tube and we would have to rush him to the hospital so it could be put back in. It was purely horrible.

> After a few more operations the tube went away and he was beginning to look normal. Today he still goes for check-ups and he has epilepsy but mostly he is a regular, annoying, bratty younger sibling. Thank God he is!

The following story, by Luke, a fifth grader, uses interior monologue to create a voice of convincing authority. By the end of this story, I had come to believe in this mirror's ability to talk to me.

How come, out of all the mirrors in the world, they had to pick me to be in a Penn Station bathroom? Why? I absolutely hate it.

The reason why I hate it so much is because of the gangs and businessmen who come in here. The businessmen come in like a bunch of wild cattle. They come in with no respect at all! None! As they come in here, they laugh like this: "Hardy har har har!" Supposedly they were laughing about some corny joke. They think they are so cool with their cashmere suits and their silk ties. But they are not cool, they are corny!

Lots of gangs come in here with their black leather jackets and weird haircuts. They smell like skunks with their so-called cologne. Sometimes with their switch-blades they carve letters into me like M.C. likes J.P. You probably think that doesn't hurt me because I am a mirror. But it really does hurt. It's like getting a deep cut on your stomach and then squeezing lemon juice on it. It kills.

If I could talk to all these people I would say: "Please don't mess me up anymore because I am already badly messed up. I wouldn't like to die a miserable mirror with carvings all over me. I would like to die happy."

One day I was minding my own business when two enemies from different gangs came into the bathroom. They started quarrelling. Then they started fist fighting. One guy started jumping around like a frog and another one started punching like a professional boxer. Suddenly the guy who was jumping got the other guy from the shoulders and threw him at me. I cracked and shattered. The gang member who got thrown into me had a bloody nose.

Well here I am. All broken. Hey! What's this man doing in here? Hey, get off me now! Don't take me off this wall! I admit it: I love it here! It's home to me! No, don't throw me in the garbage! No! Oh! No! I guess I am going to die! I am not going to cry. I sure hope I will go to the big bathroom in the sky. Here comes the dump truck. Goodbye world! Goodbye!

VOICE IN EXPOSITORY WRITING

I know a woman who found herself in the middle of a divorce. In January her soon-to-be-ex-husband asked if he might use the house one last time to throw a party. She consented, with one caveat: She requested that he and his guests take particular care with her plants. The house was filled with many species of tropical plants from around the world. He nodded wearily; he knew all about the plants. Not to worry, he told her.

She went away the weekend of his party. An hour before the party, he brought all the plants outside, in sub-zero temperature. After the party, he brought them all inside again. The plants didn't look too bad when she returned home. But within a week every one of them had died.

This nasty (I first wrote "chilling" but decided the pun worked against the impact of the story) tale comes to mind when I think of the transition we ask student writers to make from the hothouse environment of expressive writing (narrative and poetry) to the frigid air of expository writing: compare and contrast, essay, content-area writing. In trying to make this shift, many teachers have found the old cliché proven true: The operation is a success but the patient dies. The kids grudgingly make the transition, but the voice in their writing doesn't survive.

The switch from narrative to information writing does not seem nearly so traumatic for primary children. The content-based writing of young children shows a comfortable mix of information with their own zest and passion, as in this report by a first grader:

All abowt thee oyl spil *by Lauren Loewy*	*All About the Oil Spill* *by Lauren Loewy*
Some of thee ana moise did from thee oyl spil	Some of the animals died from the oil spill.
The worter wosint Blue It Wos Black	The water wasn't blue it was black.
I wish Exxon wod cleth up the Werter.	I wish Exxon would clean up the water.
I reyly fyl Mad.	I really feel mad.
and ain gry ryly ain gry	and angry . . . really angry!!!

Again, upper-grade writers have more trouble keeping some voice in their content-area writing, especially when that writing involves research. Mary K. Healy says that for older students, this genre is too often characterized by "dump-truck writing": students who pick up a clump of words (usually from an encyclopaedia), drop those words onto the paper, and are genuinely surprised when teachers accuse them of plagiarism.

Reading is a critical step in fostering voice in students' content writing. Students need to spend lots of time reading information books that are written with voice—Jean Fritz's books about the revolutionary war period; *Bugs,* by Nancy Winslow Parker and Joan Richards Wright; books by Ann

Turner and Katherine Lasky. Have students read for voice. Compare the voice in these books to encyclopaedia texts on the same subjects. Our students cannot write in a vacuum: They first need to get some image of what their writing in this area might look like.

I suggest teachers spend an hour a day for at least a week reading and rereading selected books in this genre. Students should concentrate not just on *what* the authors are saying but, more important, *how* they are saying it. Teachers might take time to help students abstract the various techniques being used: humor, rhyme, myth/truth, question/answer, diagrams, interview, fantasy. All these techniques are available for students to use in their own content writing.

Voice in writing has to do with a unique personality-on-paper. But some writers find their voice by imitating other writers. Andrew Merton, professor at the University of New Hampshire, suggests students find a journalist whose style appeals to them and imitate that writer's voice. By imitating another writer, Merton suggests, you sometimes give yourself the freedom to find your own voice. This exercise is worth considering. I know that I went through my "Hemingway period"—trying to write those lean, muscular sentences. Later, I fell in love with the irreverent and fragmentary voice of J. P. Donleavy and tried hard to write like him.

Merton makes this suggestion to college journalism students, though a teacher might try this exercise with elementary or secondary school students. Have students pick an author whose work they admire and write something in that voice. Try this with at least two writers.

But such exercises alone will not be enough to help students find voice in their own writing. A writer still needs a great deal of time to write his own work in his own voice.

In *Writing to Learn,* by William Zinsser, the author makes a fascinating distinction between two kinds of information-based writing. Type A writing transmits information; the writing has authority and expertise. Type A writing is the kind of prose teachers expect in students' finished reports or final essays. But Zinsser argues that such writing can only exist if it is supported by a great deal of Type B, or exploratory, writing. Type B writing might include learning logs, interview questions on a subject, hypotheses or guesses, diagrams, notes, maps or informal outlines.

"Our students should be learning a strong, *unpretentious* prose that will carry their thoughts about the world they live in," Zinsser says (italics mine). In other words: writing with voice. One reason their report writing so often sounds awkwardly formal and pretentious may be that we are rushing our students too quickly from Type B to Type A writing: asking them to write as experts on a subject before they have digested their ideas, before they are ready. No wonder so much of such writing sounds stilted.

It used to take me roughly five working days to finish a feature article. The first four days I'd spend reading through other articles on the subject, taking notes, generating questions and conducting interviews, revising those questions. Unfortunate friends got dragged to the local pastry shop (my treat) so I could tell them what I'd been learning. I was trying to get comfortable with all the new material: I needed time to talk about it until I could hear myself speaking naturally, with voice. On the fifth day: Type A writing. The finished article. I was ready. The article generally came quickly and easily.

Teachers might think of different ways students can do exploratory writing on their nonfiction or content-area topics. Such Type B writing should include not just what the experts say on the subject but also what *you* notice, what awes or appalls you. When Jessica, a third grader, wrote a report about the micravalve prolapse of the heart, she began by doing research. Her notes reveal not just what she has learned but also her basic reaction to the material:

> For one white blood cell—500 red cells.
> Healthy heart, blood pumps in and out. Unhealthy heart, blood drips out of heart.
> Hearts are pretty grose.
> Never become a doctor.

Jessica's first draft conveys a sense of her fascination with this condition.

> The heart is hollow and it weighs one pound. The heart sounds like this: Labump Labump. Micravalve prolapse goes like this: shushushushushu. The heart's blood pumps in and out but the michravalve's blood doesn't pump right. Hearts are icky. If I were you I wouldn't want to be a doctor. I think I should mention that for one or two of the white blood cells there's 500 red blood cells. The heart has alot of fat, the heart even has quiticells. The quiticalls look like a fat toob. The quiticalls help the heart stay in its place. The blood is really blue until ozygen hits it. When oxygen does hit it the blood turns red.

Before Jessica wrote her final draft, her teacher challenged her to take out all the "I" statements but still try to keep the lively voice of the piece intact. Jessica's final draft shows several changes:

> Do you know about the heart? If no, Labump, Labump, Labump!! That's how a heart sounds. By the way, a heart is hollow, believe it or not. The heart

even weighs one whole pound. Can you imagine? One pound in your body. Think how much the rest of your body weighs. It must weigh a lot because a heart is really small. In the *HEALTHY* heart's body, blood pumps in and out with no blood dripping. But if you have a Michravalve prolapse, the heart doesn't work right. The blood *does* pump but the blood drips. It's okay though. It's not something really bad. Anyway, this is how the blood drips. There are also two long tubes in your body. When the blood pumps into the heart, two tubes close tightly so the blood cleans and goes through the body. If the tubes didn't close, you will have dirty blood. With the Michravalve Prolapse, the tubes don't close tightly, blood drips out.

G. K. Chesterton once said: "If something is worth doing, it is worth doing badly." This is one of my favorite aphorisms. I live by this philosophy when I teach writing. It seems to me vastly more important that a student try a new technique in her writing, and use it imperfectly, than never try the technique at all.

When a student is trying something new (trying to breathe some life, some voice, into a report on Peru), we must adjust our expectations accordingly. Will upper-grade students need guidance in finding an appropriate voice? No doubt. Still, in such writing I personally prefer too much voice to too little.

Voice is far more than passion or charm; it is central to the learning process. Bill Martin has said that to really own information, to truly enter into the life of a story, poem, or novel, a child must take the words of the text and transform those words in some way. When students write with voice, they put the indelible stamp of their personalities on the information—they make it their own.

SEVEN
Beginnings

It's a funny thing about mothers and fathers. Even when their own child is the most disgusting little blister you could ever imagine, they still think that he or she is wonderful.
ROALD DAHL, *Matilda*

OVER THE LOUDSPEAKER, the principal was droning on about bake sales, bus schedules, permission slips. It was nine o'clock Monday morning; the fourth graders were pulling papers out of writing folders. Kids were chatting quietly. Kids were looking at stories-in-progress, trying to jump-start language that had been sitting cold for two days. Other kids faced the empty page. You could feel a serious silence inhabiting the classroom. One boy looked up, motioning to me with his eyes. He was bigger than the other kids, with dark scholarly glasses and a florid complexion that made me wonder if perhaps he was not wound a bit too tight. His first question seemed to confirm this suspicion.

"Mr. Fletcher," he said, "what if it's important to start it just right at the beginning? *Exactly* right. I mean, how do you do that?"

Automatically I answered Brian: "Don't worry about getting it perfect at the beginning. Don't get hung up on that. When I start writing I just try to get my ideas down. Later on I figure I can always come back and fix up the beginning . . ."

But Brian was shaking his head.

"You don't understand," he said. "I don't think you have any idea what I'm talking about."

Another uptight kid, I muttered to myself as he sighed, closed his eyes, dropped his head. He held that pose while I started moving around the classroom, talking to other kids. Ten minutes later I noticed that Brian was writing. Curiously, I went to sneak a look at his paper.

MY ADOPTION
  You would usually be born from your own mother's stomach, but not me.
  I was adopted. I was born from a teenager's stomach.

I stopped to reread those lines. Brian looked up shyly while I continued reading.

My birth mother wanted to put me up for adoption but my birth father was having a hard time giving me up. During the time when he was thinking, I had to go to a different family. They took good care of me. My birth father finally made up his mind. His idea was to put me up for adoption. The family who adopted me was Carole and Sam. . . . If I wasn't adopted, my teenage family wouldn't have had enough money for me. If I stayed with them my name would have been Harvey.

In the sixth century B.C. Lao Tsu wrote: "A journey of a thousand miles must begin with a single step." These words apply to journeys, love affairs, careers, as well as the act of writing itself. The first word, sentence, paragraph, or passage—commonly called the *lead*—represents the author's first step toward finishing a piece of writing. But the lead is more than the first step toward getting somewhere; the lead is an integral part of the somewhere itself. The lead gives the author his first real chance to grapple with the subject at hand.

Most writing is a conceptual double helix. The author writes for herself and she writes for her audience. The twin demands of inner self and external audience chase one another throughout the process of writing the story, poem, article, or play. The lead represents the author's first crack at that dual-pronged spiral of intention.

THE DRAMATIC LEAD

It's impossible to deny the power of a beginning like Brian's. His first three sentences freeze the blood, make you sit up straight. Their simple honesty seems distilled from a self-knowledge rarely found among children, or among writers of any age. Brian's story recalls a story by another fourth grader.

WHEN I GET INTO TROUBLE

Whenever I got into trouble, my mother always had a straight look at me. I would start to cry then, not out loud but in my heart.

She goes on to describe the beatings she received from her mother. When I read the story now I find myself returning to that remarkable lead, the "straight look" her mother gave her coupled with the insight that crying begins not out loud but in one's heart. Six years ago I first read her lead; I have never forgotten it. A beginning like hers grabs the reader by the throat and won't let go. Such intense honesty fuses us with the author's fate, making it impossible not to finish reading the writing.

I try a similar beginning in a Christmas story from a collection-in-progress titled *The Christmas Cactus*. The story, "The Christmas That Wasn't," begins:

"In 1974 my family canceled Christmas."

Improbable words, but true. My brother Bob had been killed in a car accident in late October; we had no patience for the holiday festivities. Four days before Christmas we packed the car and drove to a resort in the Poconos, where we stayed until the holidays were over and we could come home. We quarreled, bickered, had a miserable time. Survived.

But such leads don't always represent the penultimate way to begin a piece of writing. It is less important for a writer to find a sensational beginning than to find the *right* beginning, the appropriate lead for that article or story. Beyond the show-stopping leads described above there are many workable ways of beginning a piece of writing. I'd estimate that eighty percent of the student stories I read kick off with the words *When* ("When I was little, my father used to . . .") or *One* ("One day my grandfather took me up to the attic and showed me . . ."). It's crucial that writing teachers make students aware of the many other options available. Trying different leads can be a simple, relatively painless way for young writers to begin viewing their drafts as tentative and changeable.

STARTING IN THE MIDDLE OF A SCENE

Many writers look for a potent dose of *immediacy* to begin their writing. Writers can achieve that sense of here-and-nowness by starting in the midst of a dramatic scene. This has the effect of throwing the reader pell-mell into the action, diving into the frigid lake waters instead of tiptoeing in. Readers either sink or swim; usually, they survive.

The writer may decide to begin with a sound effect. In recent years such leads ("Crash! The baseball smashed into the big bay window . . .") became overused in many writing classrooms. Still, raw auditory clues remain an intriguing way of bringing the reader into the story or article. Katherine Paterson uses this technique to begin *Bridge to Terabithia:*

Ba-room, ba-room, ba-room, baripity, baripity, baripity, baripity—
Good. His dad had the pickup going. He could get up now.

Such beginnings are often sparked by spoken dialogue. The human voice has an alluring, insistent appeal:

"Where's Papa going with that axe?" said Fern to her mother as they were setting the table for breakfast. (*Charlotte's Web* by E.B. White)

"Yes," said Tom bluntly, on opening the front door. "What d'you want?" (*Goodnight, Mr. Tom* by Michelle Magorian)

"Did Mama sing every day?" asked Caleb. "Every single day?" (*Sarah, Plain and Tall* by Patricia MacLachlan)

These leads prick the nearly universal human desire to eavesdrop on juicy conversation. Having overheard a tantalizing glimpse into people's lives, it is difficult for most readers to put down a book.

LEISURELY LEADS

The word on leads is that they should be short. Punchy. Dramatic. Right? Not necessarily. A lead is designed to give the reader entry; often it clues the reader into what kind of writing is at hand. A thoughtful essay might start with a slow, ruminating beginning as the writer tries to nail down some philosophical axiom. An anecdotal piece about Ronald Reagan begins with a long story. Writers often decide not to jump into the thick of the plot but to begin more slowly with a description of a place, a feeling, or with a rambling introduction to the narrator or main character. Such a lead might meander through several paragraphs or even pages. Natalie Babbitt's *Tuck Everlasting* begins with a striking if oblique image that sets an oppressive mood for the story that follows:

> The first week of August hangs at the very top of summer, the top of the live-long year, like the seat of a ferris wheel when it pauses in its turning. The weeks that come before are only a climb from the balmy spring, and those that follow a drop to the chill of autumn, but the first week of August is motion-less, and hot. It is curiously silent, too, with blank white dawns and glaring noons, and sunsets smeared with too much color. Often at night there is lightning, but it quivers all alone. There is no thunder, no relieving rain. These are strange and breathless days, the dog days, when people are led to do things they are sure to be sorry for after.

Mary, an eighth grader, has written the following lead to a story, which deliberately does not "get to the point." She begins indirectly, with a mix-ture of description and philosophical reflection:

> From the overcast grey sky fell tiny white snow-flakes which fluttered this way and that until finally settling on some unfortunate leaf. Inevitably, the leaf would give out, and launch hundreds of tiny snow-flakes down onto the sledding ground where all would be smushed together and lose their unique identity. Finally, they would all be forgotten as they were assimilated by the thawing soil. A privileged few would be lucky enough to be carried back up into the clouds.
>
> "What happens when things die?" I thought curiously as I gazed out the back window of our station wagon. In front, Mom was saying something about being careful not to wrinkle our dresses. My dad would joke about my

mom's being a worry wart. Everyone would pretend to laugh and be cheerful. Gradually, the laughter subsided to nothing, leaving everyone fidgeting and self-conscious. The tension was unbearable. Only the annoying static crackle of the soft radio broke the deadly silence. We were on our way to my grandmother's funeral.

Most novice writers would have begun much more simply, perhaps with the last sentence. Mary's lead builds suspense while it creates an introspective tone for the narrative.

BEGINNING AT THE ENDING

A writer can turn a story on its head by starting at the ending and explaining how such an ending came about. Such leads play with time in a way that can be startling, even disorienting, to the reader. Such leads are often used by journalists or essayists who begin with a surprising, provocative argument and proceed to systematically lead the reader through the logic and evidence that warrants such a conclusion. The strategy can also be used dramatically by narrative writers and poets. Arthur Yorinks's outrageous picture book, *Louis the Fish*, begins:

> One day last spring, Louis, a butcher, turned into a fish. Silvery scales. Big lips. A tail. A salmon.

The author then takes us back to explain how Louis turned into a fish. Knowing how the story will end, the reader experiences Louis's transformation not with a sense of surprise but with a sense of satisfaction and inevitability at how the story reaches its conclusion.

INTRODUCING THE NARRATOR

Sometimes the writer designs the lead to introduce the character who will, in turn, tell the story. Readers who can connect with the narrator will continue reading. Certain narrators introduce themselves boldly. *Moby Dick*'s famous first sentence ("Call me Ishmael") reaches out to us like a handshake: hearty, masculine, intimate. We can trust this man and the way he reports the story. We will listen.

Perhaps no narrator was bolder than Walt Whitman in his epic poem *Leaves of Grass*, which begins:

> I celebrate myself,
> And what I assume you shall assume,
> For every atom belonging to me as good belongs to you.

Writers often use a sprinkle of humor to introduce their narrators. Humor relaxes the writer and helps insure that the writing will have voice; moreover, a narrator who can make us chuckle quickly begins to earn our trust. Marjorie Sharmat's *Gila Monsters Meet You at the Airport* begins with the narrator, a boy, announcing:

> I live at 165 East 95th Street, New York City, and I'm going to stay here forever. My mother and father are moving. Out West.

Certain narrators are anything but trustworthy. At the beginning of the story, these characters seduce us with all sorts of tricks, twitches, outrageous claims. In a story with an *unreliable narrator,* the author creates a tension between the "true" story and the narrator's peculiarly one-sided perception of that truth. This tension helps pull the reader through the narrative. Poe's short story *The Tell-Tale Heart* begins with a man on the brink of madness speaking to us in a voice choking with feverish paranoia:

> True!—nervous—very, very dreadfully nervous I had been and am; but why *will* you say that I am mad?

He explains that he had developed his hearing to the point where he could hear "all things in heaven, most things in hell." The perfect man to relate the bloody tale that follows.

The True Story of the 3 Little Pigs, by Jon Scieszka, provides an example of an unreliable narrator that is accessible to children of all ages. In this hilarious picture book the big bad wolf finally gets a chance to set the record straight. Alexander T. Wolf uses all the tricks of the unreliable narrator—humor, logic, appeals to sympathy, chumming up to the reader—as he tells his side of the story. I am not a murderer, he insists throughout this book; I have been monstrously misunderstood. The humor and subtleties of this book will best be appreciated by older students and adults.

Bruno Bettelheim argued the merits of reading children the undiluted versions of the classical fairy tales. I heartily agree. But children familiar with the original version of "The Three Little Pigs"—and who isn't—will be delighted at the wolf's transparent attempts at revisionist history.

Writing is not an exact science. One problem of a book like this is that it may encourage the categorizing and dissection of literature at the expense of the whole. Readers might get the notion that all possible leads must fit into the five or six options suggested in this chapter.

This is dangerous. There are many different ways to begin a story, article, poem, or play. Some writers begin with an intriguing generalization, a statement that provides a backdrop for the rest of the work. Such a generalization (a close relative of the thesis statement in expository writing) may suggest a central theme for what follows. Melissa, a fourth grader in Brooklyn, begins her story, "My Dog":

> Once in your life you get a best friend. Well, maybe twice. But anyway, mine was a dog. A beautiful, gray-black, glassy-eyed, curly wurly tailed, fat Norwegian Elkhound. She was beautiful.

Other strategies for leads:

* *Question:* "Did you know that the sucking power of an infant is five times as strong as the sucking power of an adult?"
* *Intriguing detail:* "My parents met in Saigon in 1968, the Year of the Snake."
* *Sentence fragments.* "A 42 year old man. A man of heart and soul."
  Or: "Expensive furs. Blubber and oil."

A tenth-grade student began his story thus: "My mother always used to say the cat had an alarm clock in his stomach, so when he didn't show up for dinner one night people started getting nervous . . ."

In which category does this lead fit? I don't know. I do know it makes me want to continue reading. When writing works, it works. Maybe we should leave it at that.

THE MISLEADING LEAD

Michael, a first grader, reads his book to the class.

"I have a farm," he says. "It has lots of animals." (He turns the page.) "Fooled ya! It's a toy farm!"

The children gasp, burst into laughter.

"Read that again!" one boy pleads. Michael beams and starts reading his book at the beginning.

Writers who explore powerful, personal subjects often begin with a "blurting lead" that tells too much too fast: "Last summer Gilly, my pet guppy, had fifty-three babies. . . ." Such leads give away the punch line of the narrative. They rob the reader of the chance to be shocked by the story in the same way the writer was shocked by the actual event.

The *misleading lead* is one way to set up and protect the surprise element in a piece of writing. Such a beginning withholds information from the reader and gives only the faintest kind of foreshadowing for the events to come. We are on tricky ground here. Writers should be very careful about withholding information. The reader may feel cheated, manipulated, and stop trusting the writer. But when the misleading lead is skillfully handled it can be a nifty way to begin a piece of writing. Take the following beginning by Pat Zibulsky, an elementary school teacher from Great Neck, New York:

> What a joy to be the lucky parent of an only child! We laugh together. We sing songs. We enjoy running mundane errands. We splash at the pool. We engage in delightful, intelligent conversation.
> Eight year old Julie has been an only child since her older sister Jamie went off to camp last week. Our normally turbulent household has settled into a peaceful rhythm. . . .

Or take the following lead to a widely anthologized short story:

> The morning of June 27th was clear and sunny, with the fresh warmth of a full-summer day; the flowers were blossoming profusely and the grass was richly green.

Thus begins "The Lottery" by Shirley Jackson. From this idyllic start, the story proceeds to gradually unveil something dark and horrible: a human sacrifice in a small rural American town.

THE AMBIGUOUS LEAD

Many of us, taking a cue from William Zinsser, among others, have exhorted students to write clearly. One writing teacher told me: "A story beginning has to be clear—you have to take the reader firmly by the hand and lead him in. You can't have the reader getting confused. Or worse: lost."

This advice is useful, but not universally true, either. A skilled writer will often use a teasing flash of ambiguity, a purposeful lack of clarity, to seduce the reader. Gwen, a fifth grader in Saratoga, New York, begins her story this way:

> From behind a tree, I saw a man-like figure lumber into the forest.

Is it a man? Is it something else? We race ahead to find out. Mark, a fourth grader, also uses an ambiguous lead:

> In most ways I am just like other kids my age.

We read on to discover that Mark has Tourette's Syndrome. The key word, of course, the word that makes it impossible for me to stop reading is "most."

The following essay of mine begins with an ambiguous lead. The key word is the unspecified "it" in the first sentence.

THE FIRST SHAVE IS THE CLOSEST

Girls know it when they get their first period. As a boy I remember watching tv with my family when my sister suddenly stood up, blushing, and ran to the bathroom with Mom close behind.

The bathroom door was shut for some time. When it opened, there was an expression on my sister's face I had never seen before. She had been gone from the living room less than an hour, but during that time an utter transformation had taken place. My mother treated her with new respect, and even my father seemed uneasy in her presence.

That evening, and for several evenings thereafter, she and my mother held long, secret talks behind closed bedroom doors. This sudden female complicity left me with only one conclusion:

Somehow, while I was watching Walt Disney on the tube, my sister had become a woman.

My transformation from boyhood to manhood was, in contrast, agonizing in its slowness. Even the leisurely swelling of my sister's breasts seemed violent compared with the almost imperceptible deepening of my voice and elongation of my bones.

Still, slow as they might be, my physical changes were terribly important to me. The thing was they never built to a sufficient peak for my father to get involved the way my mother had with my sister. My sister and I were just two years apart, but while Mom was discussing moon secrets with Elaine, Dad kept his distance from me. This worried me. I wasn't sure if I was growing up right or not.

Awkwardly, I grew through the early teens. In my sixteenth year a thin, hairy growth sprouted on my face; I was delighted when my father began to show interest in this sorry excuse for a beard. I began eagerly awaiting the day when I would get my first shave. But I was uncertain how this rite of passage would take place. Would my father give me a little booklet to read, as he had done with the Facts of Life? Or would it be something he would have to show me personally, maybe one of the few remaining rituals still physically passed down from father to son?

One spring morning my father motioned me into his bathroom and shut the door. His large presence filled the tiny room.

"I'll shave first," he told me. "You watch me and then you'll have your turn."

He needn't have said that: I'd watched my father shave dozens of times before and the process had never failed to amaze me. To watch my father shave was to witness an almost mystical transformation from beast to beauty. He began sleepy-eyed, hair in disarray, looking like a bear emerging from winter-long hibernation. Then he went to work. Shaving took him a good forty-five minutes, but when he finished his face gleamed like polished stone.

He began with an exacting pre-shave ritual: washing his hands, lathering his face, rinsing it, and then covering it over with shaving cream.

"Now you let it sit for a minute so the shaving cream can go to work softening your whiskers," he said. "You don't want to rush a good shave."

He shaved with long vertical strokes, eyes narrowed in concentration, mouth screwed up in a dazzling array of expressions—anger, pensiveness, surprise—to accommodate the razor. After finishing, he applied a second coat of shaving cream and shaved again, this time with lateral strokes. Not a single beard stalk survived this checkerboard shave. Finally, he rinsed off and applied after-shave lotion.

My turn. Mine were awkward strokes, as if I were discovering for the first time the strange shape of my face. My father's practiced hand had not left a scratch on his skin—mine was bleeding in several places by the time I had finished. He showed me how to plaster the nicks with bits of tissue paper until they closed naturally.

I ended the ritual by splashing a generous amount of after-shave lotion on my face, and experienced for the first time the surprising sting of alcohol on my tender skin.

I have shaved many thousands of times since that first shave, and my father and I have had a healthy share of father-son disagreements. But even today I still follow the shaving ritual exactly as he first taught it to me.

Nowadays I often run into guys who tell me that their fancy new razors give them the closest shaves they've ever had. As far as I'm concerned, that is just a lot of talk.

The first shave is the closest. Don't let anyone try to tell you otherwise.

EIGHT
Endings

I think the end is implicit in the beginning. It must be. If that isn't there in the beginning, you don't know what you're working toward. You should have a sense of a story's shape and form and its destination, all of which is like a flower inside a seed.
EUDORA WELTY

NICKI TOMARELLI was driving through Queens, New York. She had just eaten a big spicy lunch at an Indian restaurant, and suddenly found herself in desperate need of a bathroom. There! A Mobil gas station! She double-parked and raced inside—both bathrooms were locked. OUT OF ORDER. Nicki looked imploringly at one of the mechanics.

"Couldn't I . . . ? It's an emergency."

"Sorry. The plumbing's been all gutted."

Stumbling outside, she spotted a funeral home across the street. It's come to this, Nicki said to herself, running toward it. She stepped inside and was greeted by a very tall and menacing security guard.

"May I help you?" he asked in a booming low voice. Faced with this voice and the man's looming presence, Nicki faltered, gulped.

"Yes . . . I've come to pay my respects," she said at last.

He gave her a brief hard look.

"This way, please." He led her down a short hallway to one of the parlors. The room was deserted but for a coffin flanked with baskets of red roses at the far end. With his eyes he motioned down to an open book.

"Sign in, please."

She signed. The guard motioned that she might approach the coffin. He flanked her as she walked. The coffin was a great gleaming gold thing. The dead man was reassuringly old, white-haired, unremarkable. Nicki knelt and began to pray, apologizing profusely to God, and threw in a few good words for the deceased man's immortal soul as well. All the while, she could feel the guard's eyes on the back of her neck. She stood up and moved to the back of the room. The guard was still looking at her.

"May I use the restroom?" Nicki asked as calmly as she could manage.

"Certainly," he replied. "Down that corridor on the right."

A few minutes later she was back on the streets, breathing huge sighs of relief. She had survived.

Exactly one month later a check arrived in the mail. The check was made out to Nicole Tomarelli in the amount of five thousand dollars. It turned out that the deceased man in the funeral parlor had specified in his will that any person who attended his wake was to be given a gift in that amount. The astounded woman contacted her lawyer. He laughed and suggested Nicky deposit the check. She did; the check cleared.

Books about writing devote a great deal of time to leads, transitions, organization, but very little time to the finale: the end. In expository writing the conclusion is sometimes considered, and the writer is offered this advice: Carefully restate what has already been said.

But the ending is far more than the final ribbon that adorns a piece of writing, the rhetorical hairspray to keep everything in place. The ending may well be the most important part of a piece of writing. It is the ending, after all, that will resonate in the ear of the reader when the piece of writing has been finished. If the ending fails, the work fails in its entirety.

A common question all writers struggle with: How do I end my poem, story, article, play, or novel?

Consider this brief narrative by an eighth-grade girl:

THE GIRL
    A girl sitting alone in the cafeteria drinking her tears away while immature girls are throwing food. The girl is too scared to fight back. All she can do is ignore them.
    They surround her and make her feel miserable but they don't care. I guess those girls just don't have feelings because they are immature brats.
    They make the girl feel sometimes that life is not worth living if this is how it is going to be.
    Nobody has to take this abuse. But she does and is so scared to fight back that she goes away crying while these kids are cracking up in her face.
    There are immature brats everywhere. Some are in this school. Maybe you are one of them in this story. Maybe I am the girl sitting alone in the cafeteria. Just maybe.

I like her ending—it carries the smell of sweet revenge. She strikes back at her tormentors, and pays her way with honesty and courage. This ending, like the ending to the funeral home anecdote that begins this chapter, is a *surprise ending.* (I would have used a sub-heading but it would have spoiled the surprise!)

O. Henry, the short story writer, made a living on surprise endings. (See *The Gift of the Magi,* among others.) Readers delight in the ol' switcheroo, the impossible shocker ("His *wife* killed her?!!"), that thrill we all get when our expectations get violated at the last minute. Surprise endings are a fine and honorable way to conclude a story, film, or play.

But surprise endings are difficult to pull off. Too often, the surprise ending feels trite, contrived. A good surprise ending should never feel arbitrary; in fact, the author will quietly plant the seeds to such an ending early in the writing for the perceptive reader to discern.

"The most wonderful stories, the ones that stick with you forever, are stories with endings that are both surprising and inevitable," says Jane Yolen. "But in order to surprise the reader, first the author has to be surprised by what happens. Sometimes you think you know what the ending will be but when you get to the ending it's not there."

The writer does not necessarily aim to construct an ending to make the reader gasp (or gag). Rather, the writer tries to marry the right ending for the writing. We can help our students improve their endings by first helping them become aware of the various kinds of endings available to them.

THE CIRCULAR ENDING

In classical Greek mythology, the hero or heroine starts at home, goes out into the world, struggles to overcome great obstacles, acquires wisdom and knowledge through experience, and returns home again. This cycle of flight and return is central to much of literature. The main character—Ulysses in *The Odyssey,* Meg in *A Wrinkle in Time,* Max in *Where the Wild Things Are*—discovers that you can come home again, though you find yourself changed by the journey.

Cynthia Rylant's *The Relatives Came* begins with the relatives leaving Virginia before sunrise. After a long journey, they meet their northern kin and commence a few weeks of "hugging and eating and breathing together." The time finally comes when the relatives—now richer, fuller, and happier—must leave for their journey back to Virginia. They drive home and go to bed thinking of the next summer. The circle is complete.

The Ghost-Eye Tree, by Bill Martin Jr., also has a circular structure reminiscent of Greek myths. A brother and sister leave the safety of their house one night to fetch a bucket of milk. On the way to and from Mr. Cowlander's, the milkman, they must pass the dreaded "ghost-eye tree." The two children survive their ordeal, conquering the demons of fear and the unknown. The safety and solidity of "home"—their house and mother—take on a new significance by the end of this book.

"Poem," by Langston Hughes, provides one of the simplest and most moving examples of a circular ending:

> *Poem*
>
> I loved my friend.
> He went away from me.
> There's nothing more to say.
> The poem ends,
> Soft as it began—
> I loved my friend.

In a piece of writing with a circular structure, the reader encounters the ending-as-beginning not with a sense of "This is redundant—I read this earlier." Rather, a well-written circular ending gives the reader a second chance to encounter important material or a crucial detail that might otherwise be glossed over on the first reading. In this way it allows the reader to grasp the significance of the beginning for the first time. I suspect that T.S. Eliot may have been getting at something like this when he wrote these famous lines in his *Four Quartets*:

> We shall not cease from exploration
> And the end of all our exploring
> Will be to arrive where we started
> And know the place for the first time.

THE AMBIGUOUS ENDING

Stories cry out for resolution. We demand to know who wins and who loses, who dies and who lives happily ever after, whom she marries and whom she spurns. Yet some writers toy with this expectation, deliberately withhold this resolution, leave the readers twisting in the wind. I have ambivalent feelings about the ambiguous ending; it can enrage the reader and should be used sparingly. Still, it can be a potent tool.

Perhaps the most famous example of this kind of unresolved finale is *The Lady and the Tiger*, a short story most students don't encounter until eighth or ninth grade. A young princess has had a love affair with a virile young man far below her station. When this affair has been found out, the young man is brought before the king. Two doors face him, one with a lovely young woman behind it, the other with a ferocious tiger. He glances up. His lover, the princess, knows which is which. She looks down and gives him a signal . . .

An ambiguous ending more accessible to young children can be found in *Granpa,* a spare picture book by John Burningham that chronicles a number of small moments between Granpa and his granddaughter. Throughout the book, Granpa is identified with a green chair. Near the end of the book we find Granpa sick, sitting on this chair with blanket and medicine beside him. The last page shows the girl staring at the empty chair.

Anyone who has read this book to children knows the variety of responses it provokes. Kids look up with quizzical expressions. What happened? Where did he go? When I can force myself not to explain the ending, or push my own interpretation onto the children, a rich discussion often ensues.

"I think he's dead."

"Yeah, my granpa died two years ago."

"No, he's not dead. He just went upstairs."

"I bet he went back to Florida. That's where my grammy and poppa live."

I make a point of agreeing with any plausible response. If we take seriously Louise Rosenblatt's transactional theory of literature, we must allow students to bring their own histories and experiences to make sense of a book like this. Teachers must be extremely wary of imposing the "correct" interpretation to a poem or book. Burningham's ending exasperates some readers, but others find it roomy and liberating. The author has created a space large enough for many different readers to climb inside it, to make it their own. An ambiguous ending like this one will challenge the reader to take a more active stance toward the book, to imbue the story with the reader's own personal meanings; it will also challenge students to be able to defend their interpretations.

Jeannie Baker uses a hauntingly ambiguous ending in her book *Where the Forest Meets the Sea.* With a mixture of realistic details and fantasy, Baker brings alive the world of the Australian rainforest. The final two pages offer two very different visions for this rainforest's future: pristine wilderness or a developed resort complete with television and motels. The book ends with a haunting question—"But will the forest still be here when we come back?"—that asks students to choose between these two futures.

THE POIGNANT ENDING

How to end. Leave them laughing or crying? A small detail? A funny remark? A visual image to linger in the reader's mind?

Robert, the main character in John Steptoe's *Stevie*, spends most of the book complaining about the pesty little boy he must watch. When Stevie finally leaves, Robert begins thinking of all the fun times he and Stevie had together. The book ends with Robert pondering Stevie over his bowl of soggy corn flakes:

> He really wasn't so bad.
> He was kinda like a little brother.
> Little Stevie.

Wilbur reminisces about Charlotte at the end of *Charlotte's Web*. It takes a hard-hearted reader to resist being moved by the very last paragraph:

> Wilbur never forgot Charlotte. Although he loved her children and grand-children dearly, none of the new spiders ever quite took her place in his heart. She was in a class by herself. It is not often that someone comes along who is a true friend and a good writer. Charlotte was both.

Such endings leave a sharp emotional residue that stays with the reader when the book has been finished. The writing ends with an observation by the author, a realization by the main character, to pull together the final strands of the story. A sixth grader in New York uses this technique in his story: "A Time When I Learned the Parent's Love." (See Figure 8–1.)

Poignant endings can be quite powerful. In certain cases, the ending is absolutely crucial to understanding the work as a whole. Such endings work as the last piece of a jigsaw puzzle, without which the whole would feel incomplete.

Among published authors, Charlotte Zolotow is a master of endings. In many of her books, the various threads of the story are not woven into any coherent fabric until the very last page. In *A Father Like That*, the story begins with a boy sitting with his mother, lamenting his missing father:

> I wish I had a father.
> But my father went away
> before I was born.

Throughout the book, the boy imagines all the fun he and his father would have: playing checkers, telling jokes, visiting school during Parents' Night. The first time I read this book, I wondered how Zolotow could possibly end it. If the father did come back, it would feel like a cheap, tacked-on happy ending. If the father did not return, I would be left feeling sad. But the author finds an honest ending through the character of the mother. She listens patiently to her son and, on the last two pages, reminds him:

A Time When I
Learned the Parents Love

When I was living in Korea
I lived with my grandmother.
One day my teacher told me
that we were gonna have a test next
week. But I didn't study that
day because I thought the
teacher would give us an easy
test.
Next days I told my
grandmother about having a
test. Then my grandmother's
face turned red and said
"You better study a lot and
fast." But I didn't listen to

her. I just played baseball.
Next weeks when I got
the test. I was very surprise
because the test was very hard

Figure 8-1

I felt that I was very stupid to think that the test would be easy.

The result of the test was 52. My grandmother hit my leg 10 times with stick when she saw the score. My leg hurted very much, but my feeling hurted much more.

That night when I was sleepings I felt something or someone touching my red striped leg. When I opened my eyes a little, I saw my grandmother crying. I think she felt sorry for me, and didn't wanted to hit me. I was very happy to know that my grandmother cared me. And I felt this sudden feeling, I think it was the parent's love.

Figure 8-1 (continued)

"I like the kind of father
you're talking about.
And in case he never comes,
just remember
when you grow up,
you can be
a father like that yourself!"

THE IRONIC ENDING

We find ourselves in pretty deep water when we talk about irony, particularly with young writers. Irony is a highly sophisticated technique that lies well beyond the abilities of most young writers (or adult writers, for that matter). Irony is a figure of speech in which the actual intent is expressed in words that carry the opposite meaning. Ironic writing is characterized by restraint and understatement—a coolness in expression when the writer's emotions appear to be most heated.

Irony can be a devastating device used at the end of a poem or story. George Orwell's bleak totalitarian novel *1984* ends with the bullet entering Winston Smith's head and the sentence: "He loved Big Brother."

In the final two pages of Toni Morrison's searing and painful novel *Beloved,* the author repeats a sentence three times: "It was not a story to pass on." This strikes me as hugely ironic: When I finished that novel I felt an overwhelming need to do just that, to share the book with friends, to tell the story, to pass it on.

I often try ironic endings to my poems, such as this one about a man's doomed and delusionary feelings for a toll booth woman he encounters each morning en route to work. Is the ending too cute? Too pat? You decide.

Toll Booth Woman

I am in love with a toll booth woman.
She doesn't know it.
It is a simple affair
Strictly ruled by numbers.
I spend ten seconds with her each morning.
She demands nothing of me
Except a single silver coin.
I reach out to touch her hands:
They are always cold.
Once I brought her some gloves.
She thanked me but said

She needed her fingers bare.
Once I told her a little story—
It took me five days
To finish.
Once she broke a twenty for me
And once she broke my—what?
Faith? Heart? You decide.
I know her kind eyes have seen it all,
Princes, politicians, and priests
All reaching up to her
With money stuffed in their fists.
Yet I believe she knows who I am.
I'm the one who risks his life,
Sliding across six lanes of rush-hour traffic,
Fighting to get to her priceless
Twenty-five cent smile.

NINE
Tension

If I write what you know, I bore you; if I write what I know, I bore myself, therefore I write what I don't know.
ROBERT DUNCAN

IN HIS BOOK *Heroes,* Joe McGinnis goes in search of the American hero in order to uncover the mystique, the quintessential qualities of courage and leadership that drive such men and women. At one point McGinnis goes to the home of William Styron, author of *Lie Down in Darkness.* The two men stay up late drinking and talking. Bedtime. Styron tells McGinnis to make himself at home, have whatever he wants for breakfast in the morning except for one thing, a can of Maryland crabmeat, very special crabmeat, which Styron has been hoarding for a very special occasion.

Next morning, while William Styron is still asleep, McGinnis gets up early. Despite the late hour of the previous night, McGinnis is feeling fit, in high spirits. He bounds downstairs, into the kitchen, straight for that last can of crabmeat. Opens it. He rummages around until he finds flour, sugar, eggs. Somehow he has gotten it into his head to make a souffle, a crabmeat souffle, a dish he has never before made, never even heard of. But the idea has inspired him nevertheless.

He goes to work, puts it into the oven. A tantalizing aroma soon begins to fill the house. Not long after that, William Styron stumbles downstairs. The author's initial reaction—shock, anger—quickly melts away when he tastes that crabmeat souffle: silky, bubbly, impossibly delicious.

This tale—a kind of twisted modern version of Eve picking the fateful apple—touches an essential element of narrative: something happens. Something changes. Something goes wrong. The protagonist or main character moves through a world. But at some point, he or she will encounter trouble, resistance. Now the story becomes interesting. This is such a fundamental expectation that while we read we are always on edge, slightly tense, awaiting the first signs of calamity. We actually get disappointed when events unfold smoothly: "Nothing is happening . . ."

Tension staples the reader's eyes to the page, and writers work hard to create it. Conflict remains the quickest way of creating instant tension. In literature, conflict (as my English 101 professor explained it) falls into three broad categories: Person versus Person, Person versus Nature, and what I will call the Inner Conflict.

PERSON VERSUS PERSON

In the classic story structure, the main character has a problem (Max gets sent to his room) that usually gets worse (he sails to a distant land where ferocious monsters menace him) before it gets any better (he scares the monsters and makes it, safely, back home again). The conflict, and the way that conflict worsens, ratchets up the tension in a story, particularly when two strong-willed people lock horns.

Person versus person conflicts in many student stories go no further than arguing or outright physical fighting: pushing, kicking, throwing toys, etc. Such narratives tend to concentrate on the *what* and *how* of the conflict at the expense of the *why*. The reader rarely gains insight into the root cause. We need to explore with young writers the psychological nature of human conflicts.

War with Grandpa, by Robert Kimmel Smith, explores an unusual dispute between a boy and his grandfather. The grandfather moves into the boy's house; his inability to climb stairs makes it necessary for him to take the boy's beloved bedroom on the main floor. The boy cannot understand this; he reacts angrily with guerilla war tactics—stealing the grandfather's watch, hiding the old man's shoes, etc. The tension comes not merely from the clash of wills but also from the way the conflict gets played off against the boy's love and basic respect for his grandfather. We read fearing the worst, wondering if their "war" will damage that underlying affection and respect.

Tight Times, a picture book by Barbara Shook Hazen, begins with a familiar conflict between a young child and parents who are unwilling to let him get the dog that he desperately wants. This initial disagreement is set amidst a background of shaky financial times—second jobs, no vacations— a bleak mood reinforced by Jean Hewett's starkly effective black and white illustrations. Thus, the story gets fueled by several sources of tension. The initial parent-child conflict quickly gets swallowed up by a bigger problem when the boy's father loses his job.

I worked in one classroom in District 10, the Bronx, where the students were all boys, sixth graders, with bored, canny eyes that grew incredulous when I suggested they each try writing a picture book. They rolled those eyes, they laughed, they flopped loudly on their desks. You hear this guy? Picture books: Ha! I was ready for this reaction and pulled out three or four very powerful picture books. I read them aloud: *Faithful Elephants*, by Tsuchiya; *The Children We Remember*, by Chana Byers Abells; *Nettie's Trip South*, by Ann Turner.

The boys stopped rolling their eyes. They listened.

And they wrote well. The teacher (who confided that most of those kids had only learned a "thimbleful" all year) and I were particularly surprised by a book by Raul, a handsome boy who was already taller than me. For me, it is the narrator's distance from the conflict—the way he tries to keep above the fray—that gives the book its charm. (See Figure 9–1.)

PERSON VERSUS NATURE

In 1973 I was swimming with some college friends. This happened in the tiny island kingdom of Tonga, South Pacific, where I was spending three months on a foreign study program. A perfect beach in paradise. We stripped off our shirts and dove in. Immediately an undertow or riptide through the barrier reef started pulling us away from shore. I turned onto my back and began backstroking (my best stroke) toward the shore. Five, ten, fifteen strokes. But somehow I must have gotten turned around; when I looked up there was nothing but the indifferent vastness of water, sparkling water, in every direction. The shore was nowhere to be seen.

Panic. I fought it off, spasm after spasm. I fought off the needling voice that said: "You're gonna die." I had borrowed a pair of shorts from my friend Drew Reminganti but they were too small for me. They kept unsnapping, sliding down and tangling my legs. Three times I wasted precious energy snapping and resnapping the front. Finally, I decided to kick them off. Through the water, which was brilliant blue and deeply transparent, I could see myself. Naked. This was it. I'd been pulled so far offshore I could only glimpse palm trees and white sand when a swell lifted me up. I was scared but determined: I hadn't come ten thousand miles to Tonga to drown. I had no intention of dying, not here. Not now. It was too stupid, too pointlessly ironic. No. If it came to it, I would tread water all night long.

I was an intermittent atheist, and at first I hesitated about praying. But what the heck. Hypocrisy seemed like the least of my worries: I started praying fast and hard.

In about half an hour something shifted. I felt it: the tiniest change in the water. The current had slightly loosened its grasp and no longer seemed to be pulling me out to sea. I tried a few tentative sidestrokes, easily, to conserve energy. My heart jumped: The shore was still invisible but I was definitely moving toward it. Twenty more strokes, easy, relaxed. Now I could hear a growing and continual roar, like applause in a stadium, waves smashing onto the reef ahead. And beyond the reef—land. Terra firma. I swam toward the sound.

As I neared the reef the applause swelled to a standing ovation. Approached from the back, the waves were huge and muscular. Green serpents guarding their queen. No place to go but over the top. With a shameless inner yelp (God: help), with all my money on this ride, I lurched forward on the shoulders of the most monstrous wave I could find. The wave somersaulted me forward and flattened me under several tons of water. Underwater. My breath sealed off, I surrendered to the ocean. I surfaced, gasped, and got immediately buried by another couple liquid tons. This time when I popped up I was in waist-deep water. Standing. Standing naked on coral so sharp it cut the bottoms of my feet—I still have the scars. I cried out; I tell you I don't know if anything has ever felt so good.

A person versus nature conflict often boils down to survival: the individual's struggle to survive against fire, flood, locusts, etc. (Jack London's "To Build a Fire" is my all-time favorite story of this kind.) Unfortunately, person versus nature conflicts usually lead to ghoulish films that rely heavily on special effects: *Jaws, Towering Inferno, The Poseidon Adventure*. When such movies become the model for similar conflicts in student writing, the writing suffers a great deal.

For younger students, William Steig's *Brave Irene* is a terrific picture book for introducing the person versus nature conflict. Irene's mother has made a dress for the Countess's ball; the girl must deliver it to the Countess. A sudden snowstorm forces Irene into a journey of near heroic proportions.

The person versus nature conflict helps to reveal the harshness of the environment. But, a more important use of such conflicts is to reveal character, to put characters into a situation that tries them almost to the breaking point. Characters must find within themselves resources they never knew they had. In *Brave Irene*, readers will be awed by Irene's courage and tenacity as she fights against the snow, the cold, the "wounding wind." In Gary Paulsen's *Hatchet*, thirteen-year-old Brian Robeson gets stranded in the Canadian wilderness. Brian learns again and again to consider himself, his imagination, his observations, the most precious survival tools he has.

One variant of the person versus nature conflict is a character's first

1

To My family

2

3

4

Figure 9-1

5

6

7

8

Figure 9-1 (continued)

9

10

But not today.
I have other things
to do.

11

Figure 9-1 continued

encounter with something new that must be reckoned with: a hornet's nest, a raw oyster, or the ordinary newness of a White Castle hamburger described in the following story by Alison Chin, a New Jersey third grader:

THE WHITE CASTLE HAMBURGER

One night when I came home from New York City, we stopped to get some White Castle Hamburgers. We bought frozen hamburgers and some that we could eat in the car, and I never had one before. Well . . . you see, I bit in the hamburger, and it was really dark and I saw a green thing in my hamburger. I said, "Aaaaaaaaa, there is a green thing in my hamburger!" My brother (who always eats them) said: "Let me see." When I gave the hamburger to him he started laughing and said: "That's a pickle!" And then everyone started laughing.

INTERNAL CONFLICT

In the internal conflict (man versus himself, woman versus herself), the main character tries to reconcile opposing forces or desires. A nice example is *My Mom Travels a Lot,* a picture book by Caroline Feller Bauer in which a girl tries to sort out mixed feelings about her mother's job, which takes the mother away for several days at a time. Young readers can feel the tension in this predictable pattern book as the girl goes back and forth considering the good things and bad things about her mother's periodic absences.

Often an internal conflict does not exist in isolation but gets connected to another kind of conflict. In Tonga as I fought to stay calm, to stay afloat, I argued with myself: Should I pray or not? As the blizzard worsens, brave Irene wonders: Should I keep going or turn back? In sophisticated literature, the internal conflict often revolves around choice: free will. Internal struggles can produce unique forms of tension—guilt, worry, shame—as the character gets torn between conflicting impulses. Tell the police or keep it a secret? Return the wallet or keep it?

A story that turns on an internal conflict requires a great deal of honesty from the author, as in this piece by Aimee, an eighth grader.

JEALOUSY

"Dad." She called him dad. I couldn't believe it. I didn't understand. Dad??? It was one weekend where I went to my Dad's house. My step sister Carrie was there calling him Dad.

I guess I could admit the way I'm feeling about my Dad and Carrie's relationship. It's the way you feel when everyone else gets great presents but you get something worth nothing. Or when my brother got the bigger room.

I think I felt this way because she wasn't his daughter, and she was treated as if she were. I never had the joy of living with two parents, and she has her mom, my Dad, and she's loving every minute of it.

When I realized she was calling him Dad, all those feelings were running through my head. If I had the guts, I would have yelled right then and there: "He's not your father; he's mine."

Everyone tells me that he loves us both the same. Shouldn't he love me more? They also tell me to just ignore their relationship. But sometimes I think that's not the way to solve my problem. I have no solution, except to try my best not to get upset.

In the next piece by another eighth grader, the narrator has a conflict with his coaches and, later, his father. But the most moving parts of this story involve the boy's conflicts of conscience. This gives the prose its depth and makes this much more than just another did-wrong-got-caught-got-punished story.

During a hard-working football practice, my temper started to flare and my breath started to shorten. When it was over I went into the locker room with the intention of doing something daring or beating someone up. After I got dressed, and my breath was almost gone, I went over to get a drink of water. While I was walking out the door I purposely yanked the lever down on the fire alarm to get back at the coaches. Within seconds the alarm went off and the firemen were there.

When I went outside and saw the fire trucks, I froze and did not know what to do. I did not know whether to tell the coaches or go on the bus and go home. So I took the easy way out and went home.

The next day in school I got called down to the attendance office. Not knowing someone ratted on me, I confessed that I did it. Right away the school suspended me.

That night when I got home I was so scared to face my dad. On top of everything the worst thing about it was that my father is a city fireman.

When my dad got home that night I was scared to face him. All of a sudden I heard my dad say: "What did he do? I will kill him! Where is he?" When my dad finally got me he gave me a look to kill. If it were not for my grandma, I think I would have been on the street last night.

The next morning me and my parents had a meeting with my principal. While we were in there I was wondering what was going on in my mom's mind and my dad's mind. After it was all done, the worst part came. For the first time in my life I saw my dad cry, and that really hurt me. Seeing my dad cry—that is why I am not able to forgive myself. Also by seeing him cry, I was able to learn that my dad will always love me and forgive me for this someday.

It is not unusual to find all three types of conflict in a single piece of writing. All three kinds of tension exist in *The Ghost-Eye Tree,* by Bill Martin Jr.: the boy's continuous arguments with his sister (person versus person), his fright-ful encounter with the "ghost-eye tree" (person versus nature), and his strug-gle to control his own overwhelming fear (person versus self).

All three conflicts are also present in *Gila Monsters Meet You at the Airport*, by Marjorie Sharmat, a picture book about a boy moving from the east coast to the west. The book's tension and humor spring from the boy's stubborn refusal to move, his hilarious misconceptions about the west, and his struggle to envision his future out west through the lens of the only home he knows: New York City.

I prefer "tension" to "conflict" because the term seems more inclusive. It would be hard to define a clear conflict in Cynthia Rylant's *The Relatives Came.* Yet there is a kind of tension that slowly builds as the story pro-gresses: the pull of home. The relatives keep thinking of their grapes, back home, nearly purple enough to eat. That insistent tug of home, the fact that the relatives cannot stay forever but must finally go back to their own beds several states away, lends a poignancy to the book. The reader feels a gentle sadness as the relatives drive away.

That pull between two places—home and away—is the same one Dorothy experiences in *The Wizard of Oz. Dear Daddy,* by Phillippe Dupasquier, is a unique picture book that works off the same tension: a girl writing letters to her father who is far away at sea. On each page we see a split screen: the girl at home while her father lives a very different life on the other side of the world.

The writer can also create tension between two separate *times*—present and future, present and past. In the following narrative by Rachel, a third grader in New Jersey, the author jumps back and forth in time while writing about her dogs:

> I had two dogs: Bello and Kimmy. Kimmy was a white dog with fluffy fur. Bello was a gray and white dog with smooth fur. I remember the times they used to play together. But that day was all over.
>
> One day Kimmy couldn't walk anymore. He was deaf, too. I knew that because before when he could hear he would always come to me when I called to him.
>
> My dad once told me a story about Kimmy. Let me tell it to you:
>
> When Kimmy was a puppy someone else owned him. When she went out for a walk one day she ran into some neighbor's house and ate a whole bag of sugar!
>
> But one Friday Mom and Dad had Kimmy put to sleep. He went back where other dogs lay buried and remembered: Cinnamon, our mom's faithful dog, Kimah, our cousin's dog, and now Kimmy, the dog who was here a little while ago.

Tension might be thought of as *resistance*. Some writers create this resistance through language, in the writing itself, through the voice in which the piece gets written. What follows is the beginning of a story about a family's trip to Disney World. The reader might expect that such a story would be written with anticipation or childish delight. Instead, the author adopts a cynical, almost sarcastic voice that gives this piece a pleasing bite:

> It was a calm, quiet sunny day. I lay in a field looking up at the sky with its big puffy clouds. Then chaos started. The ground was shaking and a voice was telling me to get up. I knew that voice. Suddenly a huge crack opened in the ground next to me and I fell in. I was falling down, down through the blackness.
> Thump! I was lying on the floor of my room, annoyed that I'd been woken up from such a nice dream.
> "Sean! Get up and get dressed! We're leaving soon for Florida!" my mom's voice boomed.
> I stood up. I felt like I had been trampled on by a herd of elephants. I got dressed and stumbled down to the kitchen for breakfast.
> Ah! Breakfast. The nutritious, energizing meal which gets you ready to face the world in the morning. I walked into the kitchen to see what treat awaited me. I looked at the table and saw . . . cornflakes . . . soggy corn flakes. Dismally, I ate the cereal.
> About twenty minutes later, after getting ready, we had packed the car and were on our way to Florida. I sat in the back seat of the car next to my ten year old brother. I was surrounded by books, comics, and toys which would hopefully make the trip more interesting. My brother was cheerfully playing Gameboy and having a grand old time. I was just staring out the window, thinking about the trip. We were going to Disney world, three giant amusement parks pushed into one. This drive represented our two day trek to see a mouse, a duck, and a dog. . . .

Finally, the writer can draw on the inherent tension in all metaphors, which link or compare two things that do not seem to fit together, as in this remarkable poem by Charles Simic:

> *Watermelons*
>
> Green Buddhas
> On the fruit stand.
> We eat the smile
> And spit out the teeth.

The following poem of my own works off the tension between two places far apart, two vastly different situations, and a central metaphor that embraces unlikely things:

The Boots

After climbing Mt. Kilimanjaro
my boots were soaked, mud-clogged,
heavy as lead. I threw them out
and slept, dreamless,
     in the mountain's dense shadow.

Next morning a Masai wanderer
brought back the boots: sleek and polished,
each brass fixture snapping with light.
He had stayed up all night cleaning them
(for "the pride of work" someone later said)
and would not accept any money.

I held the boots away from my heart,
the leather soft and newly oiled,
awkwardly, no longer worthy of them,
while the man kept his silence.
I had no choice:
I gave him the boots
and flew to America the following day.

Now, years later, your curtains tremble
at the harsh words we traded,
and this coagulating darkness
where you find a queasy slumber
will not let me breathe.
I can just make out your frail spine,
the vertebrae ghostly in this dim light,
rising reluctant with each troubled breath.
You once said we all go to bed dirty,
     and wake up clean.

If you would wake right now
I would gladly stay up all night
and scrub clean our weary love
if it could be as we first knew it,
if it could once more be winged and fluid.
For I cannot trust indifferent sleep
to heal such deep and deliberate wounds.

TEN
A Sense of Place

One of the writer's best possessions is the place he knows, but without reverence for the truth about this place, he can make it into a stage set.
ROBIE MACAULEY and GEORGE MANNING, *Technique in Fiction*

PARAMUS NEW JERSEY: a consuming landscape. No less than five giant malls within a one-mile radius from my desk. A great place to buy furs, furniture, bathroom fixtures, if not exactly the most nourishing environment for a writer. If you want the truth, you should know that I'm having a great deal of trouble writing here. Not writer's block, not yet, but something else, something perilously close. Real restlessness. Clinical disorientation almost to the point of nausea.

These days, writing days, I decide to start by going for some air. Maybe a brief walk will get me off on the right writing foot. (Bad pun: see what I mean?) Breathe in the dewy spring air. Rinse the dream fragments from my head. The lawns on my street are thick, unbelievably green, billiard-table smooth. In the suburbs the men tend the lawns, and you do not mess with a guy's lawn. At 8 A.M. Wayne, the guy next door, is already at it, burly and shirtless, trimming his hedges. This man's lawn is his grand obsession. His grass defies description. Imagine a Marine's closely cropped crew top, the blades executing a close-order drill. A lawn of near synthetic homogeneity. The transition from his lawn to our lawn, with its various and sundry crab grasses, is not a pretty one. On certain mornings I can almost hear his lawn laughing at ours: haw haw haw . . .

Wayne waves me over. I am surprised; we haven't spoken in nearly a month.

"Ever get grubs in your soil?" he asks.

"What?"

"Grubs." He squints at me.

"Well, I—"

"If you do, here's the best way to get rid of them. Feed 'em grits." He grins. "They eat the grits, and their bodies swell up. Explode. I'm telling you, works every time." He grins again. "Remember that. Grits kill grubs."

I mumble my thanks and continue walking. Not a great place to write.

Very tough town for turning a phrase. Very tricky. Where I used to live, Manhattan's upper West Side, things were a lot easier, at least on this score. Writing there was a legitimate way of life. The bookstores and coffee shops were thick with novelists and freelance journalists, poets and playwrights. The joke was that if you accidentally shot off a gun you'd kill three writers. Famous writers, too. Some days I'd actually glimpse old Isaac B. Singer slowly making his way up Broadway to his favorite little coffee shop. Seeing that, I'd smile, gulp my coffee, hurry home to write.

The setting, or place, creates the world in which the characters live and struggle. In this world, the plot will unfold. Something will happen.

In *The Art of Fiction,* John Gardner describes good writing as a "vivid and continuous dream." This is a useful definition for all kinds of writing: bad writing is anything that jolts the reader out of that dream. The reader must make a leap of the imagination to connect his world to the world of the writer. The writer who can create a believable world, a convincing place, goes a long way toward trancing the reader into the larger world of the article, biography, poem, or story.

Young writers typically pay little attention to setting. This is true whether the writing is set in familiar terrain (backyard, attic, grandmother's house) or in an exotic locale (a trip to Montana, a panda bear lumbering up a slope in the Himalayas, Martin Luther King sitting in his prison cell in Selma, Alabama). A boy writes a story, "My Trip to Maui," but if you snipped off the title you would find very little "Maui" woven into the story. It could just as easily have taken place in Brooklyn, Florida, or western Massachusetts.

I usually start writing with something I know: a detail, an image, a snatch of overheard conversation, a story, a person. A place. Place is an excellent starting point because places live in the deepest parts of us. In one sense, we never leave them: We soak them up, carry them around, all the various places we have known.

"It is by the nature of itself that fiction is all bound up in the local," Eudora Welty has said. "The internal reason for that is surely that feelings are bound up in places. . . . Location is the crossroads of circumstance, the proving ground of 'What happened? Who's here? Who's coming?' "

Clam digging is a world I know. I spent three long summers digging littleneck clams on the Great South Bay off southern Long Island, New York. By itself, clam digging is not enough of a story, but I might use this setting for any number of pieces of writing: poems, stories, a novel, a feature article on the disappearing baymen on Long Island.

Clamming was a tough, fascinating world. I might start trying to animate this world by describing the clamming artifacts: our Garvey (a twenty-foot long boat with a flat deck). Rakes and tongs. The burlap bags we used to store the clams. The cull rack we used to sort saleable clams from seedlings that had to be thrown back. You'd dump a pile of clams onto the rack and shake vigorously. The legal littlenecks and cherrystones would stay; the seed clams would fall through the irons.

Routine. We left the dock each day at 7 A.M. and worked until mid-afternoon, or later, or earlier, if we pleased. We made our own hours. We'd drive the boat a half hour into the bay, secure the anchor, take out the tongs, and begin work.

My brother Jim and I were tongers. We worked in water just eight feet deep. The clam tongs were a giant pair of scissors. There were two long wooden handles attached to a basket with sharp teeth three inches long. You'd stand at the edge of the deck, drop the tongs overboard while holding onto the handles, open the tongs, jam them down, work them closed, lift up, shake out the mud, listen for clams. If you heard some, you'd lift up (keeping the basket closed or you'd drop the clams), dump them onto the deck, take a short step down the boat, throw in the tongs, start again. In this way I'd work my way down one side of the boat while my brother worked the other. We might harvest a bushel and a half in a day, maybe more. We got paid every day, cash, by the wholesalers on the dock, some of whom weren't above shorting us a few dollars if we didn't speak up. I earned around thirty-five or forty dollars each day; I had a number of teen-aged friends who regularly earned over a hundred dollars a day.

Odd fact #1: Mornings, the offshore wind would usually be mild, but after lunch a fresh, cool breeze would blow out of the south. The One O'Clock Chop. It happened every day precisely at one o'clock; the old-timers said you could set your watch by it. You could see the breeze roughening the glassy waters over toward Fire Island as the breeze moved toward you. When it arrived, you could watch all the boats swing around on their anchors until everyone was pointing south, into the wind.

Odd fact #2: The veteran clam diggers, the baymen who clammed year round and not just as summer work, each had a single seagull who perched on their boats. One seagull per boat, same seagull every day. I observed a complex symbiosis between these men and their birds. The seagulls would eat the cracked clams on the deck; sometimes the men would break open clams for the seagulls. What did the baymen get back? A mascot, I suppose, and meager companionship. I greatly admired the true baymen, tried hard to befriend them, and dreamed of one day having a seagull come land on my boat. But the baymen scorned me, and so did the seagulls. My brother and I clammed alone.

I would start describing this setting with my five senses.

Touch: the noon heat, the horseflies, the blisters on my hands and the salt water that made them smart. (The job wreaked havoc on the hands. Some nights I'd wake up with my hands cramped up, knotted together. My brother would have to help me pry them apart.)

Smell: the dank, rotting smell on the deck from all the muck and crabs and seaweed we dredged up from the bottom of the bay.

Sight: girls on their sailboats a few hundred yards away, a few light-years away, smugly smiling as the skimmed past en route to Fire Island.

Sound: boats droning, clammers shouting friendly obscenities at each other, the heart-stopping sound of a mother lode of clams rattling in the tong basket when you shook it up and down.

Taste: clams on the half shell, unimaginably fresh. We'd bring out lemons and Tabasco sauce. For lunch we'd eat a couple dozen clams harvested just moments before.

In the following story, by a California second grader, the author uses three of her five senses to describe a pristine setting:

> I love wild animals. and one time I went to a caben. and the caben was on a rocky slpe. every day me and my brother climbed to the very top. we edmired the gloryes vue as we listened to the morning glores sing. it was very soothing to listen to them. and it made me warm inside. so every morning we did the same. it was a brilyant way to start my day. and it put me brother in a good mood. and it made every thing good. there was a stream that shimered. and the sunlight shone beautyfuly on the distant sparkles. it was great to have so many wonderful things at one caben and it was better to just go alone as I looked at all the wonderful things around me and listened to the beautyful sounds. as I hung my feet in the stream it trickled over the shining rocks. it made me feel away from every thing. when it was time to go I was sad but you can't go on dreaming for ever.

This author does not let her spelling problems prevent her from taking huge risks with language. One senses a young writer working hard here as she tries on a language of beauty and awe. I also sense that this place is a haven where she can find refuge from other problems.

Jerry Watson has made a useful distinction between *backdrop* setting and *integral* setting. Backdrop setting is simply an arbitrary place in which the story takes place. Backdrop setting has little or no effect on the rest of the story. Watson says: "The integral setting, on the other hand, exerts a great deal of influence on the values, speech, and actions of characters, the movement of plot, and the presentation of theme and mood."

I would want the clam digging world to be an integral setting for whatever I was writing. For example:

A brutally hot day. Windless. Every time we set the anchor, the boat starts drifting in a new direction.

"Which way are we going?" Jim snapped.

"Nowhere," I mumbled.

Or: One day it was so hot, the horseflies so thick and ornery, we bagged and rinsed our clams (just a peck each), pulled anchor before lunch, headed for the beach. And wouldn't you know it? We ran smack into my father.

Or: Just before lunch, with a loud flutter of wings, a seagull landed on our boat. At least we figured it for a seagull. It was an old bird, with feathers the color of dirty dishwater. She had no beak. We didn't care. We were delighted, named her No-Beak, and immediately set to cracking open a dozen tender seed clams for her enjoyment, all the while moving carefully, cooing softly, praying she would not fly away.

Unless I am writing a realistic travel piece, I'm not interested in describing the clamming world unto itself. Rather, the setting exists as another element in the whole story.

"Only in cheesy realistic novels are places described for their own sake," says novelist Robert Cohen, author of *The Organ Builder*. "The setting gets described to further what the book is about—the characters, the theme. The setting is always expressive of something more than itself."

The setting can be used in many ways in a piece of writing. A brief description of a place is an excellent way to set the scene at the beginning of a piece of writing. (Carson McCullers uses this technique to begin *The Member of the Wedding*.) An initial description can have a function similar to a foyer in a large house; it gives the reader time to become at home, to "feel the ground" of the story before walking into the real action. I use this technique to begin the following story:

> I park my car close as possible to the building. It is morning, biting cold; I move quickly from the car toward the school building. There is a narrow ribbon of warmth that surrounds school buildings in the winter, a sweater of heat perhaps two feet wide, fueled by heating vents, boiler steam, convection from the windows. I hug the walls trying to stay within this warm zone as I hurry to the front door.

The setting can also be a fine way of building tension in a piece of writing. I don't mean just the It-was-a-dark-and-stormy-night kind of tension, but also the taut pull (or push) between opposing forces:

> I meet with teachers in the All-Purpose Room, actually a combination science and music room. Bongoes and tambourines sit in uneasy proximity to pinned arachnids and pickled mice embryoes. On the wall, a plaque of BUT- TERFLIES FROM AROUND THE WORLD has been placed not five inches from a large and elaborate diagram showing various musical notations. As the teachers and I talk, a bitter, lacquered smell rises to my nostrils. I can't quite tell if it is formaldehyde or the gleaming varnish on that huge African drum. . . .

The setting provides the author with an excellent way to develop character. The relationship between character and the character's physical world is a complex one: the harsh American West shaped the settlers who, in turn, cut down the forests, built communities on rivers, killed buffaloes, pushed Indians off their lands. This interrelationship lies beyond the reach of most young writers. What they can understand is this: Each of us is a product of the world we live in. Botanists and zoologists tell us that a true understanding of any species requires that the species be studied not in isolation but within its native environment. The same is true for humans. The world we live in sculpts our psyches as well as our bodies. (Professional clammers tend to be barrel-chested, with huge arms and thick weathered hands.) Jean Craighead George explores the relationship between character and physical environment in *Julie of the Wolves:*

> Miyax was a classic Eskimo beauty, small of bone and delicately wired with strong muscles. Her face was pearl-round and her nose was flat. Her black eyes, which slanted gracefully, were moist and sparkling. Like the beautifully formed polar bears and foxes of the north, she was slightly short-limbed. The frigid environment of the Arctic has sculptured life into compact shapes. Unlike the long-limbed, long-bodied animals of the south that are cooled by dispensing heat on extended surfaces, all live things in the Arctic tend toward compactness, to conserve heat.

An experienced writer can uncover the subtle links between character and setting. Not only does environment shape character but the character's emotional state determines how he or she perceives the environment. The blue sky glows like some gorgeous sapphire or stretches like some dreary barren desert depending on how we feel at that particular moment. The skilled writer will use the way in which a character perceives a setting to give the reader significant clues about that character's state of mind.

At the end of his book *The Art of Fiction,* John Gardner suggests several writing exercises. I believe such exercises should be used sparingly with children, if at all. Still, there is at least one intriguing exercise involving setting as a way to reveal a character's state of mind:

> Describe a building as seen by a man whose son has just been killed in a war. Do not mention the son, war, or the old man doing the seeing. Then describe the same building, in the same weather and at the same time of day, as seen by a happy lover. Do not mention love or the loved one.

"A sense of place" does not necessarily mean a large place. "Place" could be small as a closet, a drawer, the inside of a wallet. Consider the following description of a car's interior by Rebecca, a fourth grader, and notice how well it gets at the mood of turbulence and disarray that is really what the story is about.

> During the protest for the homeless people, we were always rushing here and there so Mom got lots of tickets for parking in the wrong places. She'd just throw them onto the floor of the car and drive away. Whenever we got in and out of the car we'd step on those parking tickets. After awhile the tickets got trampled in with all the coffee cups and spilled coffee and napkins and wrappers and newspapers on the floor of the car. Pretty soon they got so soaked you couldn't even read the date on the tickets. A little while longer and the tickets got moldy and you'd smell that moldy smell whenever you got in the car. It wasn't long before those tickets start *disintegrating* right under your feet. Finally we couldn't stand it anymore. We cleaned out the car. But that moldy smell never really went away.

Consider also the following short story by a fourth grader. This piece of writing does many things well, utilizing successive flashbacks to quickly catapult the reader back in time before returning us to the present. I am most struck by her ability to evoke the two settings in the story, and by the tension between them:

WHISPERS IN AN OPEN FIELD
Chapter One: A Frightening Event
"What!?" I couldn't believe it was happening. Here I was standing in front of millions of people (or what seemed like millions of people). My mother crying silently with her head tilted. Her small, pale fingers clutching a white lace hanky. My dad in a blue suit looked encouragingly at me. Mrs. Taylor's face streamed with tears under lace, black veil. Everyone was looking at me. Expecting "me" to say something!
"Ah . . . well . . . " What was there to say?
I'm at the moment on an altar looking into the faces of all these strange people.

My best, best, best friend, Elizabeth Taylor, had died because of me. But wait! Don't blame me. Listen.

It happened last month. Elizabeth had come over to play. Her favorite game was just to kick a ball around. It was my turn. I kicked the ball hard, too hard. It rolled into the street. I told Elizabeth to go get it and kick it back. She ran to it. As she ran, an orange car sped out of its driveway and smacked into Elizabeth. It knocked her down against the pavement! She rolled down towards a stone a little bit and stopped.

I remember the terrible screech of the car, the hideous scream I had shrieked and the sound of Elizabeth's leather jacket rubbing against the pavement. It was horrible.

Chapter Two: A Secret Place

Yes, it was true. Elizabeth was dead. The words kept ringing in my head. But there was something else that kept blinking in my brain. The field. It was a wonderful place. My favorite place in the world. Elizabeth's too. I suppose that's why we chose it. You see, when Elizabeth was alive we used to go to this open field. It was deserted, but kept very clean. The grass was always sparkling green, and in the middle of the field was a gazebo. Actually, it was only a weeping willow tree, but it "wept" to the ground, if you know what I mean.

The reason we chose it was because we needed a quiet place, a clean place, and a deserted place. A place for what? you might ask. A place where two girls could grow into friendship.

Chapter Three: Telling It All

The place was for secrets. I suppose that I will not go there any more. Elizabeth and I made an oath: "Neither of us shall go to the field without each other." I was certainly without Elizabeth. And even though the willow branches whisper on, our secrets stay protected under the spring leaves.

"Hurry, Julie!" my mother was calling. I hate to tell you where I was going. Elizabeth's . . . fune . . . funeral!

I was purposely trying to be late. I didn't want to see Elizabeth dead in a wooden box. And I didn't necessarily think Mr. and Mrs. Taylor wanted to either. So what was the point of a funeral?

"You were great, dear!" my mother said.

Gee, I thought. All I did was say: "Elizabeth meant a lot to me." I was too embarrassed to say any more. I guess I should get Elizabeth out of my mind. I'm not going to ever think about death and funerals again. But my memories will always live. The field, the secrets, the tree, the oath, the rustle of leaves. The whispers.

ELEVEN
A Playfulness with Time

And so we beat on, boats against the current,
borne ceaselessly into the past.
F. SCOTT FITZGERALD, *The Great Gatsby*

TIME-WISE, the writer faces a dual challenge: how to handle the element of time in one's writing but, even harder, how to handle time in one's life. Specifically: how does a writer find time to write?

The writer does a remarkable thing. She spends time, often a great deal of time, on something as peculiarly intangible as a poem, an essay, a stretch of prose. She works on it gradually, house by house, block by block. Over time she may build an entire city of words. For what purpose? To acquire new knowledge? Get paid? Get published? Improve her physique? Meet fascinating people? End up with a gleaming piece of art to adorn her living room? Not likely.

We may be able to envision the sudden burst of energy required to clean out the garage, to confront that friend who inexplicably never phones anymore. We may be able to imagine blowing a large sum of money on a fancy car or new extension on our house. But who can fully imagine the staggering daily investment of sheer time required to become a skilled writer?

Ideally, the writer has an abundance of time because quite often when a writer sits down to work, nothing happens. No words or ideas come forth. This sort of frustration comes with the territory. Writers learn to factor writer's block into their time.

"Over the years I've developed the self-image of a shopkeeper," the writer Amos Oz says. "Mainly it's my business to open the joint at a set time, to sit and wait. If I have customers, it's a blessed day. If I don't, well, I'm still doing my job."

Several years ago I was given that rarest of gifts: time to write surrounded by time to waste. I was invited to spend one month at Yaddo, a writer's retreat in Saratoga Springs, New York. Heaven: a giant mansion set on four hundred pristine acres. The daily ritual at Yaddo never varied. Breakfast from eight to nine. After breakfast each writer or visual artist would pick up a lunch box and head off to a private studio to work. We worked every day from nine until four in the afternoon. Dinner was at six. Such vast stretches of time felt disorienting and, at first, lonely; by four o'clock I'd be starving for the sound of a human voice. (There were no telephones or televisions in the studios.) But I wrote a ton. More than the lack of interruptions, it was the lack of even the *threat* of interruptions that made Yaddo a place where you could really get work done.

Most of us never get to experience a Yaddo. Back on planet Earth, few of us have any sustained stretches of time to write. For most of us who write, or yearn to write, time remains the greatest scarcity—more than money, space, or energy.

Today, May 28, 1991. A writing day. I had it all planned. I would work on this chapter from 10:00 until around 2:30. Robert would take his regular nap from 10:00 until noon. JoAnn would go to work at noon; I had arranged for a babysitter to watch Robert from noon until 2:30.

My plans crashed and burned. The first sweltering day of the year; Robert sweated, fussed, refused to nap. Feeling sorry for the little guy, I caved in, drove to Toys R Us, and bought him a little plastic Cookie Monster pool. By the time I had finally got it home and wrestled it into the backyard, Robert had fallen asleep. Sleeping Robert = Prime Writing Time. But it turned out that the pool had a small hole in the bottom. I brought it back and stood in three long lines, fuming, until I could exchange the pool for another model.

Back home, 12:35, I started writing, but got interrupted by four phone calls from different banks. We were in the process of shopping around for a mortgage; I felt compelled to take the calls. All the while I was trapped in this cliche: the grains of sand slipping through the hourglass. No time to write this chapter about time. Another unfunny joke. Finally, I started to write again, but all the while I was listening for baby Robert, sleeping Robert, a slumbering time bomb of a Robert, ready to go off at the slightest ring of the telephone or loudly closed door.

This is the perfect excuse for not writing: no time. But the real writer refuses to fall for it. Writers write. In notebooks, on napkins, at the kitchen table surrounded by dirty plates.

I know a Cambodian man who was very poor in his youth. There was barely money for food, let alone paper. He was in love with a young woman from the neighboring village. He would get up before sunrise, sneak down to the riverbank, and write her love letters in the wet sand. She would read them when she came down to wash clothes in the river later that morning.

In our culture relatives, visitors, spouses, children, and salesmen are famous for devaluing the writer-at-work and often feel no hesitation about interrupting the writer on the slightest pretext. Many writers compensate by becoming almost fanatical about protecting their time. (I know of one man who, upon hearing his son screaming outside his office from a fairly serious head wound, tersely reminded his wife through the closed study door: "I'm not home. I'm not here. You take care of it.")

This may be going too far. But writers write. Writers find a way to get it done. Consistency matters. Never a day without a line. Hemingway tried to write about two hundred and fifty words a day. That doesn't sound like all that much, but if you write two hundred and fifty words every day you'll have a completed book by the end of a year.

Donald Murray says: "I am surrounded by neighbors and friends who want to write and know more than I do, have more to say than I do, are blessed with more talent than I have, but they do not yet have the writer's habits."

Of all the writer's habits, consistency may be the habit that matters most.

In a classroom the teacher decides the frequency and duration of student writing time. But for young writers, handling the issue of time in the writing itself can be very difficult. From my own observations in classrooms, the problem boils down to this: Inexperienced writers are typically controlled by the element of time in their stories.

Why? JoAnn Curtis suggests that young children may lack the language connectors ("The summer before . . ." "The next day . . .") that might allow them to shape the contours of time in their stories.

It also seems to me that timelessness is an intrinsic part of childhood. Most kids I see don't keep track of time. They don't measure it the way adults do, don't parcel it out, save it. A boy sorts and resorts his baseball cards, first by team, then by position, then by batting average. Hours pass: by adult standards a colossal waste of time. But children are not adults. The river of time that runs through them is deep, strong, unbroken. When I encourage my own children to make the transition from timelessness to time planfulness, I am aware that I am asking these children to begin moving out of their childhood.

Children have trouble controlling time in their writing because they simply do not see it as an element to control. They are oblivious of it. I wonder if this unawareness does not get reinforced by the (over-?) emphasis on personal narratives in many writing workshops. Too many young writers develop a narrow conception of writer-as-reporter, whose sole task is to provide a faithful recounting of events the writer has experienced. The much maligned "bed-to-bed" story results from the writer's inability to exclude any moment, no matter how trivial, from a particular day.

Here is a crucial discovery about time for a writer: *The experience and the writing that is based on that experience are not the same thing.* The real-life subject, and the writing based on that subject, exist as two distinct entities. Often the two are only loosely linked, connected (and distorted) by the writer's imagination.

Writers who draw on their own experiences for their writing must constantly juggle the demands of what really happened (who/what/when/where/why) with what needs to happen in the piece of writing to make it work.

The distinction between *real time* and *story time* probably has certain developmental limits. It has been my experience that most first- and second-grade writers want to include complete lists of events. In a writing conference, when I suggest they focus their writing on a particular "slice of the pie," primary grade children tend to decline my invitation. But once a writer can uncouple real time from story time (perhaps in third or fourth grade) the writer can begin to perceive time as just one more element—like character or setting—that must be considered in a piece of writing.

We might encourage young writers to move toward a *playfulness with time* in their writing as an alternative to linear time. By "playfulness" I mean a sense of time as the mind plays with it—fretting about a future event, dwelling on a past slight—as we move through a series of present moments during the course of a day.

I am mowing the lawn of our Durham, New Hampshire, home, just smelling the grass, enjoying the tight reverberations from the motor running up the handle to my arms and shoulders (PRESENT). When I finish the backyard, Adam and Taylor set up a sprinkler and start running through it. Their squeals bring me back to one summer afternoon when I was ten (PAST) and my uncle lit off a firecracker. I was standing further back than anyone else, but a tiny piece of rock shot into my right arm. . . . Thunder rumbles (PRESENT), and I start thinking about the cookout planned for later on (FUTURE). If it rains, where on earth will everyone sit to eat? The lawnmower sputters (PRESENT): Is it out of gas?

A writer can handle time in many different ways: cutting it, bending it back, stretching it out. With a complex element like time, there will always be a danger of mentioning rather than really delving into the issue. Teachers of upper grade or secondary students who want to dwell on the element of time might consider a deeper exploration with:

- Examples from literature (see Appendix)
- Examples from student writing (very important—probably more important that literary examples; it is my experience that a strategy does not become part of the "class culture" until students see their peers using that strategy)
- Direct instruction

LINEAR TIME

Linear time, or chronological time, is the modus operandi for writers of most ages. There is nothing wrong with this; in fact, most teachers would consider *sequence* a strength in a piece of writing rather than a weakness.

I see two kinds of linear time showing up in student writing. Sometimes time does show up in a story, but it is time wound very loosely:

> We went to Chuckee Cheese and we had fun. We played lots of videos and I found two quarters. Then we had pizza and soda and cake. I helped Anthony open his birthday presents. . . .

In a story like this, events follow one another in a kind of "and next" fashion. (If we parallel Jerry Watson's distinction between two uses of setting, we might think of this as "time as backdrop.") There is some evidence of sequence—in the Chuckee Cheese ritual, video games do precede the soda and pizza—though the events are not closely linked together. We might think of this as a sort of "Greatest Hits of the Day" story, with events placed in the right order.

A more sophisticated kind of story sequence occurs when events are shown to *cause* other events, as in the following story by fourth grader Sylvia:

> As I stepped in the car crying my mother said, "It'll be fun in preschool." While driving to school mom explained what I was going to do.
> Soon-e-nuf we were there. We walked stair-by-stair and hall-by-hall. Then we stopped in the room. Five years olds screaming and jumping all around. There was a big box. I wanted to find out what was behind the box. But I still wanted to go home. I turned back to ask mom to go home. She was running down the hall, half way to the door. MOM COME BACK! PLEASE! Now I was running after her. When I was half way down the hall I tripped. I bruised my knee but the pain didn't bother me, all I wanted was mommy to come back and bring me home. It was no use.
> The teacher brang me back in the room. I sat down. Things were flying around in my head. Why did I have to fall? What couldn't I cry louder? I was stupid. But I survived the day, and found out what was behind the box.

Sylvia's story is truly driven by sequence—events are intricately woven together. The girl is crying *because* she has to go to school. Her mother reassures her, brings her to school, and tries to sneak away. Seeing her mother leaving causes the girl to panic and, ultimately, to hurt herself. (Incidentally, the story has both a recurring detail and an ambiguous ending that seems perfect: since we never find out what is in the box, it comes to represent school itself.)

SNAPSHOTS

Readers expect sequence in most kinds of writing. Even a biography usually ends with the subject's death. But some authors violate that expectation by deliberately removing the element of time and providing the reader with *snapshots* of a particular world, place, or character.

In *When I Was Young in the Mountains*, by Cynthia Rylant, a girl reflects on her childhood memories of Appalachia. The element of time is largely absent in this book, though it does lurk in the background. We know that events in the book happened in the past. And some pages are linked together (first the children heat water for their bath—later they shiver as they drink hot cocoa). But most events in the book are removed from any kind of linear sequence. The very lack of sequence helps to give the book its timeless quality and its charm.

The writing of primary children often has a snapshot quality, however unintentional, when they write "all about" pieces. Older and more sophisticated writers might take a closer look at this technique for their own writing; the snapshot strategy can be useful when writing an informal character sketch.

FLASHBACK

Tomorrow is Labor Day. The Fletcher Clan will gather, will eat, laugh, sing. But mostly we will reminisce, telling stories of the good old days. This tendency to be pulled into the past is deeply rooted in human nature. The flashback is a simple way for a writer to revisit the past in a piece of writing. Most flashbacks utilize a structure that is nearly circular. They begin in the present, go back to the past, return to the present, and then continue through the present.

A flashback can come at the very beginning of a book (*Sarah, Plain and Tall*) or in the middle (*A Chair for My Mother*). It can encompass a very brief moment (*Hatchet*) or something quite long. In Jean Craighead George's novel *Julie of the Wolves,* the entire second section of the book is a flashback on Julie's unhappy and failed marriage.

A flashback can go a long way toward illuminating the present. The flashbacks in the story at the end of the previous chapter help explain the narrator's precarious emotional state.

The picture book shown in Figure 11–1 was written by Tamiko and illustrated by Aisha, both sixth graders in New York City. It's interesting that while Tamiko's book deals with an unpleasant subject, divorce, her flashback recalls happier times. The difference between those good times and the divorce creates a satisfying tension in the book. For me, even more than the girl's reunion with her father, the flashback carries the highest emotional moment in the book. The close-up of the three ice cream cones (the bigger the issue, the smaller you write) poignantly evokes a time when the family was intact.

OMISSION

We need to let our writers in on a simple writing secret: You don't have to include every event that happened. You can leave stuff out. You *should* leave stuff out.

A young man nervously prepares for a first date. The writer begins this story by describing him carefully shaving, picking out a shirt—no, too fussy—and putting it back, finding another one, checking the clock, checking his wallet. He takes a deep breath and leaves his apartment. Must the writer describe this young man walking to the subway station, buying a token, waiting for the train? No.

> . . . He looked in the mirror one last time, took a deep breath, and stepped out of his apartment.
> He found her name in the long list beneath the row of mailboxes on the buzzer: C. Terranova. He pressed it, and the loud buzzer made him jump. The doorman eyed him suspiciously. . . .

In other words, a lengthy description of how he got to her apartment building, which train he took, etc. is unnecessary. The writer may *decide* to include it—to build suspense or to reveal a character's state of mind—but it can be omitted. The reader is fully capable of accounting for the time between leaving his apartment and buzzing her apartment. Such omissions are crucial if the writer is to grasp the next strategy.

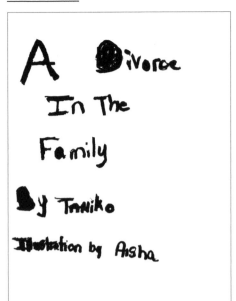

1

For children
All over the
World

2

When Tamiko was four
her mother and Father had a
divorce. Nothing was working out
for them.

3

She didnt cry because
she didnt know what
was going on. Yet she
still asked what had happened
to her daddy. Her mom would
try to change the subject.

4

Figure 11-1

Her parents did have some good times and bad times.

5

She would think of some good times.

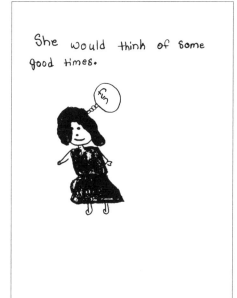

6

And say I remember the time we all went to Central Park.

7

Daddy would put me on the swing.

8

Figure 11-1 (continued)

And when the icecream truck came daddy would buy three icecream cones.

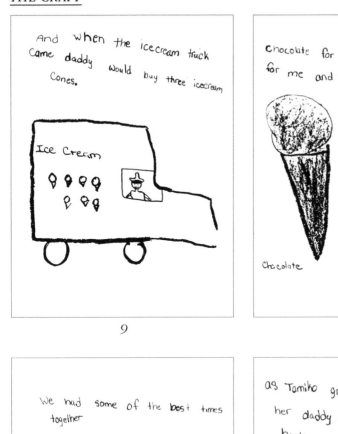

9

Chocolate for mommy, Butter Pecan for me and strawberry for him

Chocolate   ButterPecan   Strawberry

10

We had some of the best times together

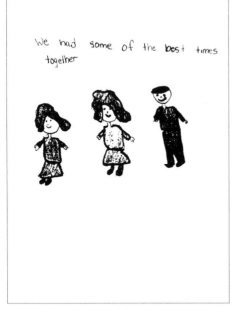

11

As Tamiko grew up, She realized that her daddy was never coming back.

12

Figure 11-1 (continued)

Then one day the phone rang. Her mother picked it up. Tamiko was wondering who it was.

13

When her mother got off the phone she had a smile from cheek to cheek.

14

Tamiko begged; who is it? It was your father. He want you to go to his house every weekend. He said he will come and pick you up tommorow which is Saturday.

15

Tamiko was happy because now she could have more good times with her father.

16

Figure 11-1 (continued)

FOCUS

We need to teach students how to write small, not just in terms of detail (the blue veins on the back of my grandmother's hands) but also in terms of moments, time. In *The Beach Before Breakfast*, a picture book by Maxine Kumin, the narrator gets woken at dawn by a friendly man. The child and man lose themselves in the magic of exploring the beach, finding shells, seeing sandpipers, so much so that the book's end comes as a shock: time for breakfast! The entire book takes place in the very earliest part of the day.

I am leery of prewriting exercises, classrooms where each student is required to complete one before starting the writing. However, a simple map or timeline may help students stand back from their experiences and gain a degree of detachment from the element of time in their writing, particularly when it comes to *focus*.

One summer day when I was about eleven and my family was on vacation, at the beach, I met another boy named Bruce. We started palling around together the way kids do. We dug a huge seawall together to hold back the high tide. Within an hour, without talking all that much, we became quite close. It wasn't a hurried closeness (though we both knew we would likely never see each other after that afternoon), but in that short time we developed a sympathetic vision. I could see the world through his eyes, and it was a bright and glorious world. I think he could see something similar through my eyes. We ate lunch in a sand fort we had made. A few hours later we said goodbye. When he walked away I knew I was seeing the last of my best friend.

A timeline of this experience might look something like this:

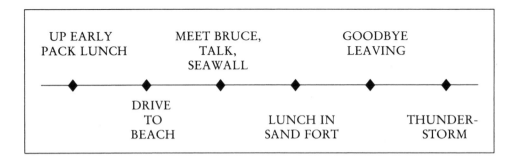

The crux of this day was the time spent with Bruce. If I circle just that part of the timeline and omit the rest, I can begin to sense the story taking shape in a new way.

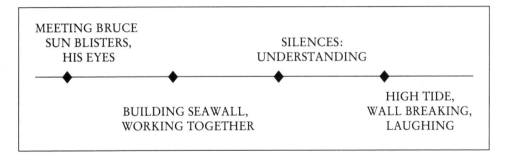

MEETING BRUCE
SUN BLISTERS,
HIS EYES

SILENCES:
UNDERSTANDING

BUILDING SEAWALL,
WORKING TOGETHER

HIGH TIDE,
WALL BREAKING,
LAUGHING

Focus does not mean writing shorter pieces. The crucial aspect of focus is that getting narrower allows the writer to go deeper, to get under the surface of a story by delving into one particular part of it.

Writing about a single, narrowed duration of time is only one kind of focus. A writer might also focus time by looking at repetitive time: habits, rituals, traditions. In Rylant's picture book *Birthday Presents*, for example, two parents tell a little girl about her real birth day, and then tenderly describe each birthday that followed. We might think of this kind of time focus as vertical rather than horizontal.

SLOWING TIME

Young writers tend to give equal attention to each part of a story:

> We came to school but we were only there ten minutes before we got on the bus again! We took a ride. The bus stopped at MacDonald's and we had breakfast there. I couldn't eat all my pancakes. Then we got back on the bus. It took almost an hour to get to the zoo. There was a line so we had to wait to get in. First we went to the lions and tigers. I felt sorry for them. Next we went to the House of Primates. An orangatang bit Brendan on the finger. Our teacher flipped out. One of the mothers bought us ice cream. We had hamburgers for lunch. In the afternoon . . .

This story was written by a third grader. The writer is remarkably fair: he gives equal time to the breakfast stop at MacDonald's, the long line, Brendan's accident, etc. There is little sense that one event might be more important (and deserve more space, more words) than the others.

I sense that Brendan's accident with the orangutan represents the "hot spot" (to borrow a phrase of Karen Howell's) in this story. A note of caution: As teachers we cannot presume to know exactly where the hot spot lies in students' stories. What may seem important to us may be of little interest to the writer, and vice versa. But once the student has identified the hot spot, we can suggest ways of slowing the writing. By slowing time, by lingering at the crucial moment, the writer helps the reader to discover the relative importance of various events and characters in the writing.

One of the most effective ways of slowing time is to write a dramatic scene. First, however, the writer must clearly understand the difference between dramatic scene and narrative summary.

> Last night my father came home and told us he'd been fired. We were all shocked. He stayed up til after midnight talking to my mother about it. When I went to bed I was so worried I couldn't sleep.

This narrative summary typifies much of the narrative prose written by students: controlled, distant, passive. In such writing, the narrator plants himself squarely between the reader and subject. All the story's information, all its raw materials, get filtered through (and, in many cases, deadened by) the narrator. Here the reader has no other evidence that "everyone was shocked" except that the narrator says so. In a dramatic scene, the narrator tries to give the reader a direct experience of sights, sounds, and events:

> When Dad walked in the door, his tie was open; his shoulders were slumped.
> "Hya, Dad," I said, but he didn't seem to hear. He put his briefcase on the kitchen table and looked through me.
> "Your mother," he said at last. "I need to talk to your mother." He started walking toward the stairway.

Richard Price compared the difference between a dramatic scene and a narrative summary to the difference between being at a stadium for a baseball game and reading the box scores of the game in the newspaper. Real fans would always rather be at the game, hearing the crack of the bat, smelling the hot dogs. . . .

The dramatic scene is a powerful tool that can do many things:

- Slow the action
- Introduce dialogue and gesture
- Make the narrator an active character rather than a passive storyteller
- Allow the reader to experience the grief/delight of the story at the same time the narrator does
- Give readers the raw materials of the story so they can infer larger issues

In a movie, the director chooses carefully where to use slow motion to draw out a crucial scene. This technique usually comes at the film's hot spot—farewell kiss, reunion, winning touchdown catch. A director would never film the entire movie in slow motion; the technique would quickly lose its novelty and become tedious. In the same way, a writer would not write a whole story in dramatic fashion—unless, perhaps, she was writing a play. A good narrative should have a *balance* of scene and summary. The writer thinks long and hard about which part is crucial enough to render as a dramatic scene.

Those of us who teach writing need to take the time, through our own reading and writing, to become sensitized to how time is handled in texts. Even with our help, young writers will have trouble with this element of writing. Time is tricky—even professional writers have a great deal of difficulty with it. Writing teachers need to be alive to the tiniest breakthroughs their students make—even accidental ones—toward a more fluid, playful sense of time in their writing.

The story in Figure 11–2 on the following pages was written by a kindergarten child in Queens, New York. As you read it, and enjoy the intimate voice, also notice how well this young writer plays with time: first building suspense, then lingering, then jumping into the future.

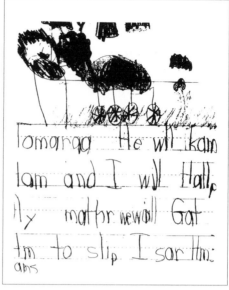

1. My baby is a cry baby and is so cute. I love him so much. His name is Tal.

2. Tomorrow he will come home and I will help my mother. We will get him to sleep. I saw him three times.

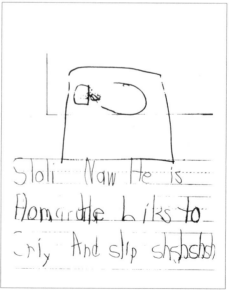

3. I am ready for him. His carriage is ready. I will pull him in his carriage slowly...

4. ...slowly now, he is home. He likes to cry and sleep. Shhhhhhhhhh...

Figure 11-2

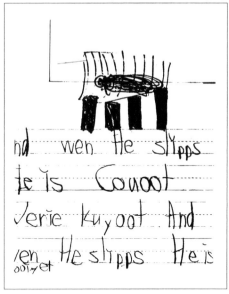

5. Shhhhhhhhh When he is sleeping I play because he cries so much. And I help my mother.

6. And when he sleeps he is cute, very cute. And when he sleeps he is quiet.

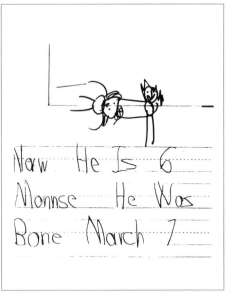

7. I help my mother. And when my mother nurses him I play.

8. Now he is six months. He was born March 7.

Figure 11-2 (continued)

TWELVE
Unforgettable Language

The bags under his eyes were pouches containing the smuggled memories of a disappointing life.
GRAHAM GREENE, *A Burnt-Out Case*

WHEN I WAS a senior in high school, my mother had a baby: Carolyn. While it was great being that old and having a new baby sister, it was plenty tough leaving a three-and-a-half-month-old when I went off to college. I missed her. I wrote to her. When she was two, I shaved off my first failed beard, stuffed those whiskers into an envelope, and mailed that beard to her. I have always felt that my relationship with Carolyn was special; I'm her oldest brother and, as I'm still fond of reminding her, godfather.

When I came home from college Carolyn wanted to play with me. I usually had other fish to fry: work, sports, movies, sometimes even a date. One day, when Carolyn was four, I tried to explain it to her.

"Look, I can't, how about tomorrow? I'm really busy today."

She flounced away and looked back at me, frowning hard.

"The minute you come home," she said severely, "you put on the cloak of busy-ness!"

This book would not be complete without a chapter that at least touches on beautiful writing, truly original language, images that make you sit up straight when you're reading.

In *The Relatives Came*, Cynthia Rylant describes how the house felt different at night with relatives sleeping all over the place: "It was different with all that new breathing in the house."

A sentence like this makes me start talking to myself, repeating it over and over. A sentence like this made me want to be a writer in the first place.

Writers have particular other writers they go to for inspiration. They read the words of the masters over and over, awed, forever relearning the trade (how does she *do* that anyway?), thrilling to the power and beauty of language in the hands of a gifted writer. Such "writerly writers" represent a select club. Thomas Mann, Virginia Woolf. For Raymond Carver: Anton Chekhov. For Cynthia Rylant: James Agee and William Maxwell. For me:

Vladimir Nabokov, Annie Dillard, and most recently, Martin Amis, who seems incapable of writing a stale sentence. His prose crackles with originality: "You can kill time in a number of ways but it always depends on the kind of time you're fighting: some time is unkillable, immortal" (from *Money*).

But you don't necessarily have to go to professional writers to find original language. In this respect I find myself taking inspiration from very young children. Some children seem to speak a kind of unschooled poetry, however unintentional or inaccurate. Hearing them, I understand why Romantic poets like William Wordsworth believed that "the child is father to the man."

Words come alive in the mouth of my stepson Adam. I am startled by what he says as much as by the way he says it. For the past few years I have used my journal to record his best one-liners, his pithiest aphorisms.

Adam, four years old. I give him a huge yellow leaf I found in the woods. "Look," he exclaims. "A primary color!"

Adam at five. He loves the bath, but hates getting out of the tub. He stands there, shivering. "Quick, Ralphie, wrap me up!" he cries. "I'm soaking cold!"

Adam coming down for breakfast: "When I woke up my eyes were like two eggs cracking open!"

Listening to music, Adam points at the radio: "I'd like to be *in* there, right in there with that music."

Adam eating pizza with a topping of black olives: "Hey, there's a blizzard of olives under here!"

I ask Adam to clean his room. But when I get upstairs the room looks messy.

"What are you doing?" I ask, giving him a strong suspicious look. Across the room, he squirms and laughs.

"Stop it, you're tickling me with your voice!"

With JoAnn pregnant, it has begun to dawn on Adam that he will no longer be the youngest child. You can see him trying to figure out his new place in the family. Yesterday Adam, JoAnn, and I went out for breakfast. JoAnn and I were talking about throwing away some of the junk in our attic. Adam listened closely.

"Would you ever throw *me* away?" he asked, dead serious.

"Absolutely not," JoAnn said. She looked at Adam, at me, and back to Adam, "We love you much too much for that."

"That's a rule," Adam said seriously, lifting his index finger for emphasis. "No throwing people away."

I have watched Adam trying to figure out my role as stepfather. Usually he is the first one to wake up, but one morning I have to go into his room to rouse him. I rub his back, singing softly: "You are my sunshine, my only sunshine." He gives me a tender, frowning look.

"I'm not your sunshine," he says softly. "I'm your son."

One more Adamism that is famous in my family. When Adam was about four years old, my mother took him for a walk.

"Take my hand," she said. "We're crossing the street."

"I know, Grandma," Adam said. "You *are* getting old."

As a writer, I admire Adam's language tremendously. I admire his fearlessness, his expansive playfulness, the fluidity with which he puts images together. Who would think of putting "blizzard" next to "pizza"? An odd image, but it works. Maybe all images that sound new are essentially odd. The expression "soaking cold" is not commonplace, yet we all know exactly what he means.

The spoken language of young children makes me think of molten lava: steaming, flowing, magnificent. Their written language can be that way, too, with images that take away our breath and allow us see the tired old world with new eyes.

"Smoking is like eating fire." John (third grade)

"The wind makes raindrops curve when they fall. When they fall on the ground they self-destruct." Lauren (second grade)

"The sun was spraying rays of light all over." Alison (third grade)

The moon
A monster's eye,
The stars
His shiny teeth . . .
    Jenny (second grade)

Later, however, when children learn the proper conventions, it seems that their language cools to safe correctness. With older children it's rarer to see the same degree of freedom, the bold images and striking metaphors, that we see with younger children.

Why? It may have something to do with the expectations adults have for children's language as they mature in school.

"Most schools are about teaching conventions," JoAnn Curtis says. "We don't value experimentation as much as correctness. We've broken out of that box a little bit with skills, inventive spelling, but not yet with language. We don't look for the surprise in language—we look for language that gets the job done."

We start creating an environment that encourages original language by *expecting* mistakes. When I work with children, I keep a sharp lookout for those words, phrases, and sentences that are "wrong but wonderful":

"I'm sorry, Adam, but I can't seem to put this Ninja Turtle thing together," JoAnn says.

"But Mom," Adam protests, "it explains it right in the destructions!"

Most of us would smile at such an error. We appreciate Adam's courageous attempt at pronouncing such a big word, how "destructions" is also a three-syllable word that rhymes with "instructions," the way his mispronunciation touches on another kind of truth about children's toys. We are not worried that Adam's sentence is not "right" because we know that it is on the way to being right. In the meantime, the error strikes me as more interesting than the right word.

"Will you please behave?" an exasperated mother tells her son.

"I *am* being *have!*" the boy retorts.

Garp's son feared the "under-toad" (undertow) in *The World According to Garp* by John Irving. The same boy used to say that his mother was going to "gradual school." My stepson Taylor used to ask me about the "World Serious" when he was five.

In Figure 12–1, the poem by Daniel, a first grader at PS 178, the Bronx, has one word that is "wrong but wonderful":

"Swiffeling," of course, is not a word, though it seems to me that it *should* be a word. In fact, it sounds like the perfect word for the peculiar way shadows move across a wall. Writers have been known to make up a word where none exists. In *The Ghost-Eye Tree*, Bill Martin and John Archambault concocted the word "foolie" to describe those scary thoughts that bedevil your mind when you're walking in the dark.

It is tempting to take the position that some children are simply born with the ability to write truly original language, while some are not. Seven-year-old Andrew Park, a student in Lisa Lenz's class in Caldwell, New Jersey, read Langston Hughes's poem "Long Trip." The poem moved Andrew to write a poem about the sea (see Figure 12–2).

In the poem shown in Figure 12–3, Vanessa Hawkins, a second grader in Sea Cliff, New York, takes on the persona of a star. Her poem challenges

Daniel   Dec: 61,- 1987.

Shatossoszi   in The diro

Shatossoszi in The diro

Swaofinllin all   ova   my

wall   on to   my llap

like a hoss   jimpbin.

Figure 12-1

Shadows in the air
Shadows in the air
Swiffeling all over my wall
Onto my lap
Like a horse jumping

the   sea   is   a

Young   child   learning

How   to   write

and   all   he   ~~Seems~~

to   write   is   W²s

Figure 12-2

the old song that advises you to "catch a falling star and put it in your pocket."

Certain kids do seem to have the knack for poetic expression. But I strongly believe that original writing can be taught, or at least fostered. Writing teachers can do several things to help children revitalize the language in their writing. First, we need to attune the ears of young writers to magical language wherever they hear it—in books, poems, the writing of their peers, talk.

One student remembered this snatch of conversation with her father one morning and used it to start her story:

> "C'mon," her father said. He shook her. "UP!"
> "What time is it?" she mumbled, staring out the dark window.
> "It's o-dark-thirty," he said crisply. "Time to rise!"

We must also beware the curriculum cliches that creep into our classroom, those shortcuts that help us to categorize at the expense of exploring ideas in depth. We need to find new ways to say old things—and this takes work. For example, in this chapter I deliberately avoided using the words "fresh language," a phrase used so often it has lost the newness it must have once had.

Here is one strategy for writing in an original fashion: *write what you see, not what you are supposed to see.* Art students learn the same thing. The

Stars
we twinkle in the
cold sky air we are there
all night if you try to
pull us down we will
burn a hole in your pocket.

by Vanessa Hawkins.

Figure 12-3

brain takes the discordant images of the world and organizes them into the coherent and familiar things of our worlds: house, moon, bus, comb. A writer learns to present images *before* they have been reorganized and homogenized:

"My father's head was floating in the hot tub."
"The moon was tangled in the oak tree's branches."
"A dark tarantula of keys lay on the kitchen counter."

We know, of course, that the moon is a quarter million miles from earth; still, it *looks* like it gets caught in the branches of the tree. That might be an original way of saying it. I knew that the entire body of my father was floating in the hot tub, but I could only see his head. This unreconstructed image makes the sentence come alive in a new, if somewhat surreal, way.

We need to be aware of those moments when students create powerful images of their own, when they use language to boldly extend their thinking. Thomas wrote a story that begins:

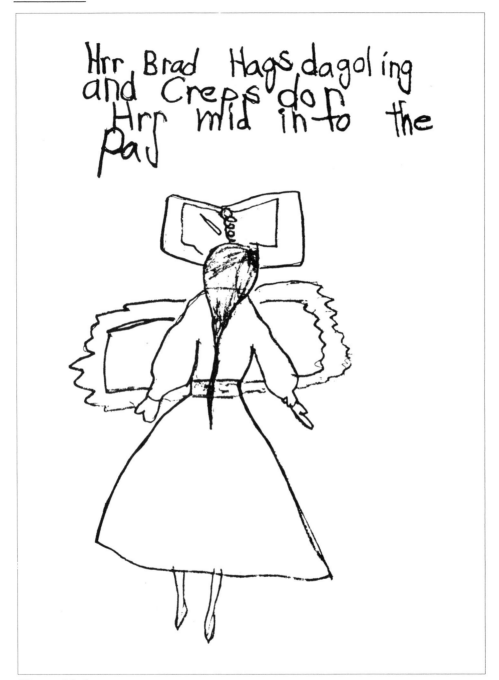

Figure 12-4

Her braid hangs dangling and creeps down her mind into the page.

Many, many years ago, in the Southwestern United States, there was a very beautiful forest. It was so beautiful and famous for its splendor that before you entered it you had to genuflect. . . .

The use of "genuflect" is surprising, possibly even offensive to some people; still, it represents a bold and original attempt to communicate the sense of awe and reverence engendered by this forest.

Startling language can give the reader a dazzling jolt of recognition (literally: to re-think), as in the poem by Erin Spampinato (see Figure 12–4), a six-year-old in Lisa Lenz's first-grade classroom in Caldwell, New Jersey. One day Erin was idly watching her best friend lying on the rug, reading. The girl had a braid that hung down onto the book. Suddenly it looked to Erin as if the braid were an actual link between brain and book. This image inspired Erin's poem "Meghan"; I don't know if I have read a better one about reading.

THIRTEEN
A Significant Subject

*Look at your feet. You are standing in the sky. When we think of the sky,
we tend to look up, but the sky actually begins at the earth. We walk through
it, yell into it, rake leaves, wash the dog, and drive cars in it. We breathe it
deep within us. With every breath, we inhale millions of molecules of sky,
heat them briefly, and then exhale them back into the world.*
DIANE ACKERMAN, "A Natural History of the Senses"

I ONCE TOOK a writing course from novelist Gail Godwin. In a soft
North Carolina drawl, she spoke to us about how each writer must find the
right idea to write about.

"Too often a writer picks an idea that turns out to be nothing more than
a *solander*," she said.

We looked at her blankly. Solander?

"A solander is a book-object," she explained. "Tell me if this has ever
happened to you. You're at a party at someone's house, and you choose a
book from a bookcase. But when you take it down and try to open it up,
there aren't any pages. It's not a book at all. Instead, you find some object
inside—a cigarette lighter. A silver flask."

We nodded. Certainly, we had seen them. And it gave a certain satisfaction to learn that *solander* was the precise noun for these imposters. But
what did that have to do with choosing a good idea to write about?

Godwin anticipated this question by reading aloud from *Technique in
Fiction*, by Robie Macauley and George Lanning:

"Learning to write sometimes seems like a succession of waste motions,
and among the most wasteful is that one which urges us to commit to paper
a fiction which—though it may look solid enough, though it may even be
bought for publication—is as hollow, as much a trick, as those boxes which
people make by cutting out the center of a book and gluing together the
edges of the pages. These are called solanders, and few are the writers who
have not perpetrated a fair number of solander-fictions in their time."

"Can you give us an example of a story idea of yours that turned out to
be a solander?" someone asked.

Godwin smiled and, a bit reluctantly, began relating a story. Her chilling
tale is probably not appropriate for elementary school children. I'll leave

that to the discerning reader to decide. Still, it left enough of a lasting impression for me to try to reconstruct it here.

One Saturday morning, Charles returned home from doing some errands. He walked into the kitchen and found Ranger, his big Doberman pinscher, writhing on the floor in the strangest way.

"What is it, boy?" he asked, bending down and checking him over. Ranger's mouth was open; the dog seemed to be having trouble breathing, though there was no blood or wound of any kind that Charles could see. What was wrong with him? Frantically he picked up the dog, carried him to his car, and raced down to the office of his veterinarian. The vet reassured him that he would telephone as soon as he could figure out what was wrong.

Charles drove home. While he was unlocking the back door, he heard the phone ringing and ran to pick it up.

"Hello?"

"Charles?" The veterinarian's voice.

"Yes. What's wrong with Ranger?"

"Listen carefully," the vet said, "and do exactly what I say. I want you to hang up the phone and leave the house. Immediately. You don't have a moment to lose. Call me as soon as you're safe."

"But—"

"Just do it!" The vet hung up. Charles left the house. He drove to a small diner a few blocks away. Inside the restaurant, Charles's hands were shaking so hard he dropped the coin twice before finally jamming it into the pay telephone slot. It rang only once.

"Charles!" the vet said. "Are you all right?"

"Of course I'm all right. Why? What the hell is going on?"

"Listen. I found out what was wrong with Ranger. Are you sitting down? I reached down his throat and found three fingers lodged there. Three *human* fingers. Do you hear what I'm saying, Charles? Your dog was choking on a man's fingers."

"My God!"

"Someone must have broken into your house while you were out. Ranger must have attacked the man and, well, you get the picture. Whoever did it could even be there right now, wounded and dangerous. If I were you, I'd take a deep breath and phone the police."

Godwin stopped telling the story. We were silent.

"What happened?" somebody finally sputtered.

"I don't know, I never finished writing it," Godwin said, shrugging.

"But it's such a great beginning!" I said.

"Somebody told me this—it's a true story, supposedly—and it did seem like an intriguing premise for a short story. But when I started writing it, I discovered I couldn't do it. It was a solander, for me, at least. There was that one chilling detail, the Doberman pinscher choking on a man's fingers. But when I started to write, it seemed like a gimmick to me. Beyond that the story didn't really go anywhere. I abandoned it."

For the purposes of this chapter, I'm going to define a solander as any topic that seems promising at first but which turns out to be hollow, empty, barren. There can be many reasons for this. The writer may not care about the topic. He may have no knowledge of it. He may be unable or unwilling to get close enough to the subject to write with honesty and clarity.

The solander trap is a real one. On several occasions I have tried out subjects that later revealed themselves as solanders of the highest order. I actually finished a bad novel whose main character was named William Billy. (His buddies called him Billy Billy. Get it?) Another awful novel idea—a futuristic world in which women were the oppressors and men had to fight for equal rights, etc.—I abandoned after a few weeks.

Readers bring to any piece of writing a number of expectations. The first one is *intelligence. Insight.* Before style, before technique, we are drawn to writing that challenges our intellect. We demand pages and paragraphs and sentences that make us think. Readers are selfish: We insist on being enriched by whatever we read. We want to go somewhere we've never gone before. The skilled writer works hard to bring intriguing, engaging ideas to any topic—in any genre—he or she writes about.

This cannot be stated bluntly enough: The writer must have something to say. It may seem strange to find such an important chapter near the end of this book. The truth is that all the preceding chapters are meaningless unless the writer can find something interesting and important to say about the subject. It doesn't matter if a writer begins it cleverly or ends it neatly, organizes it smoothly, writes it dramatically, writes it with voice. The "it" itself has to have merit.

A first-grade teacher passes around pieces of paper.

"I want you to think of any important ideas you might write about," she tells the kids. "You can write those important ideas down on the paper."

When she hands a piece of paper to Michael, the strongest writer in the class, he frowns up at her.

"I'll need a couple sheets," he says. "You know my letters are still pretty big. I can't write too small."

"Fine," she says. "You can have all the paper you want."

But instead of writing, Michael just sits there.

"What's wrong?" his teacher asks, kneeling beside him.

"See, I'm not sure I understand what you want us to do," he says. "Do you want us to write ideas that are important—or ideas that are *significant?*"

Michael's precocious question, the distinction between important and significant, seems worth exploring. It's important to begin with the realization that there is little inherently interesting about any subject. Depending on how it is handled, a subject can seem lively or it can put us to sleep. The sole difference lies in what the writer brings to the subject at hand. It is not the subject itself that will hold the reader but the writer's relationship to that subject. Our best writers find significance in subjects that might seem terminally boring. David Owen, a writer whose work appears regularly in *The Atlantic,* can make mundane topics (Barbie dolls, the history of Xerox machines) positively sing when he writes about them. I'm not very handy, not much intrigued by the construction of a house; still, I could not put down Tracy Kidder's book *House.*

Consider this brief narrative by Bob, a sixth-grade student.

THE ROOFERS CAME BACK

Yesterday the roofers came back to do another roof. Last time they were here my cat died. They dropped a big piece of roof onto one of the piles. The crash scared my cat into the road. It wasn't their fault but I always think it was.

This time I want to keep my cat inside but she likes to go outside a lot. When I came back from school yesterday, I felt like pulling the ladder down while somebody was on it or when they all were on top of the roof so they couldn't get down.

Bob's piece of writing does not begin on a promising note. "Yesterday the roofers came back to do another roof." (So what?) But the flashback allows this writer to dig into his subject in an unexpected way. By the end we understand the significance of this subject to Bob. The image of the roofers is used by the author to indirectly get at the real subject—his anger and sorrow at the death of his cat.

I seek a subject to write about with two distinguishing characteristics: it must interest me and it must be something I think I can write well about. Actually I'm often not sure I can write well about it, but if I'm sufficiently intrigued I'll give it a try. Over time, a writer learns which subjects have real writing potential and which do not. My own best subjects seem to be those that anger, appall, baffle, or exasperate me. I look for a subject with *resonance:* that internal echo you hear when you thump it.

For me, a significant subject is usually connected, however loosely, to my life. This seems to be true not only for a story or poem idea, but also when I'm seeking a nonfiction subject to write about.

It has been said that the trick to being a successful freelance writer is to specialize: music, medical breakthroughs, the parent-child relationship, etc. Specializing saves time: You don't have to take a crash course on a new subject every time you write a new article.

Alas, I have not specialized. Instead I have published articles about Al Oerter (Olympic gold medal winner in the discus), bartering, buying a franchise, computer screen glare, the Museum of Natural History, lithographer Tatiana Grosman, the Animal Medical Center in Manhattan, Harrods of London, a quadriplegic doctor.

In each case, my original fascination with the subject had seeds in my own life. Both Tatiana Grosman and Al Oerter were residents of West Islip, New York, where I was living. (I often watched Oerter, benevolent giant, pass our house on his morning runs.) I used to visit Harrods frequently while taking corporate tours to London.

One day, at the beach, I noticed that the wife of a close friend had a rose tattooed on her leg just above the ankle. I asked her about it; the question unleashed a long passionate reply about her tattoo. I had never before been interested in tattoos. But listening to her story, I found myself leaning forward. This conversation led directly to an article I wrote for *Cosmopolitan* about professional women who get a small, tasteful tattoo on their bodies.

This seems important. Students who find themselves writing dispirited prose on any subject might look harder at themselves and ask: Where do *I* stand on this? What's *my* point of view? Forget what the experts say: What part amazes or angers *me?*

Too many students write on issues or subjects they know nothing about. While professional writers—and some amateurs—can care about almost any subject through sheer will, this feat lies beyond the reach of most writers. If we sense that students are writing about topics they don't know or care about, we might suggest they try another idea, something closer to the heart.

I don't necessarily look for a subject about which I am already an expert. Total expertise can be as dangerous as total ignorance. Inside experts with *too* much knowledge of a subject typically produce the worst writing in many technical subjects (cameras, computers, insurance). Such writing is notoriously opaque, voiceless, filled with jargonese.

A healthy dose of ignorance is often helpful when you begin researching a subject: It keeps you honest, it keeps you humble. It insures that you will be a learner. It gives you room to expand into the majesty or the heartbreak of whatever subject you are writing about. It provides room for the imagination which, as the writer Bruce Brooks has pointed out, flows from what is known to what is not known.

I start with this axiom: In most ways I am very much like everyone else. I figure if I can make something understandable to myself, I can make it understandable to my readers.

FACTUAL INSIGHT

Insight may be communicated through the facts a writer digs up. Writers fill notebooks with odd facts, tidbits, statistics, and tuck these factual nuggets, raisin-like, into the loaves of their writing. For instance, at the time of Robert's birth, my journal contained these facts I will use one day:

- Many babies are born leaking milk from their own breasts. This is sometimes known as "witch's milk."
- Rarely, a baby is born with the amniotic sac still intact. This is known as being born "in the caul."
- An infant's suck is five to ten times as strong as the suck of an adult.
- Studies show that a baby can see light from within the womb.
- During the birth process, two separate bodily systems insure that the baby's brain continues to get an uninterrupted supply of oxygen.
- After birth, in some Polynesian cultures, the placenta is placed in the earth along with a tree sapling. After nourishing the fetus, the placenta nourishes the baby tree.

These facts are not invented or imagined; they are drawn directly from the actual world. In one sense, the writer acts as a teller-of-secrets. I try to dig up lots of facts, though I know I will not necessarily use them all in any article. Rather, I will select the best facts from among them. Murray has written about how skilled writers work from abundance. "It takes thirty gallons of sap to make a gallon of maple syrup; it takes hundreds of pages of notes to make one *Reader's Digest* article."

An article in 1991 about hurricanes, by Bob Shacochis in *Harper's,* is studded with intriguing facts about hurricanes:

- An average hurricane precipitates approximately 2 billion tons of water a day.
- During every minute of its life a full-blown hurricane releases energy equal to a hydrogen bomb.

Diane Ackerman's book, "A Natural History of the Senses," is replete with provocative nuggets of fact:

- The average body has about five million hairs.
- Massaged (premature) babies gain weight as much as 50 percent faster than unmassaged babies.
- "In Japan, chefs offer the flesh of the puffer fish, or *fugu,* which is highly poisonous unless prepared with exquisite care. The most distinguished chefs leave just enough of the poison in the flesh to make the diners' lips tingle, so they know how close they are coming to their mortality."

In an unpublished short story of mine, "Friday Night at the Spider Fights," I had enormous fun writing one passage filled with delicious facts I had collected about spiders:

> Coop knew spiders the way dentists know bad breath—I mean he *knew* them, inside and out. He taught me that there are 30,000 spider species in the world. The 650 species in New York and New England alone equal the number of bird species breeding in all of North America north of Mexico. The biggest spider in the world is the "bird-eating spider" (*Theraphosa*) of South America. They found one with a body three inches long with a ten inch leg span fully extended. That's a lot of spidermeat for a starving man. The smallest spider in the world is the *Patu marplesi* of Western Samoa, found in moss at an altitude of 2,000 feet. It measures about half the size of a printed period (.) The fastest spider in the world is *Tegenaria atrica.* This spider has been clocked at 1.73 feet per second, or 1.17 mph. That may not sound fast, but it is a speed of 33 times its body length per second, compared to the human record of 5 1/3 times its body length per second. Our spider, Antaeus III, was a *Tegenaria domestica,* close relative of the fleet *Tegenaria atrica....*"

Facts can be illuminating; however, facts alone will not suffice. Too much dense information can sink the writing. Facts need to be interspersed with narrative or anecdote, the information humanized through humor, voice, and wit. Consider this report by Blake, an eighth grader from New York.

THE FIRST DEAD PERFORMANCE

When I recently visited the Tower of London in England, I heard a very interesting story from a tour guide at the site where stood the scaffold on which two of Henry VIII's wives were executed, Ann Bolyne and Catherine Howard.

To understand this story one must know that there was an entire ceremony to having one's head chopped off. First, you would stand on your scaffold and give a speech, thanking your relatives for being there, and explaining what should be done about your body and possessions. While the above ritual would be of dubious importance today, it was considered in poor taste and altogether dishonorable if one insisted on being carried kicking and screaming to the axeman. Following that, you would tip the executioner. In fact, this is where the word "tip" comes from today. It stands for the words "to insure promptness." The higher the tip, the faster, and less drawn out, would be your end.

One day the Duchess of Salisbury was scheduled to be executed. After her speech, she tipped the executioner a sterling silver tea set. This was the equivalent of a year's worth of salary for an executioner. As the Duchess knelt down by the block, everything seemed just dandy, for such a macabre setting. However, unbeknownst to everyone present, the executioner was only an apprentice, and this was his first live execution.

At the grim moment we can imagine the nervous young axeman winding up, perhaps his tongue hanging out in concentration. Suddenly, he brought his axe down in a shining, whirling arc . . . and missed. He actually hit the lady's shoulder. Hell hath no fury as one who receives less than his or her money's worth, especially in this instance. The old woman leaped up and began a long catalogue of personal remarks about the executioner's family. While she was in this state, the axeman took an unexpected swing at her. She ducked. Then she panicked. She began running around the scaffold like a chicken deprived of its head with the axeman swinging his axe to and fro, running behind her. He missed her a total of seven times before her head finally came off.

Although you may think this a morbid example of humor, it is a very good idea of what the old English thought to be funny. It does generate a certain amusement and, besides, keep a stiff upper lip, as the English might say.

Blake's report is entertaining, written with a lively voice that makes it a pleasure to read. But the report also contains a number of what the detectives call "hard facts." The reader feels informed and enriched to learn the origin of the word "tip," for example. Without this historically accurate information, the piece would not be nearly so effective.

INTERPRETIVE INSIGHT

In the end, the reader expects more from the writer than juicy trivia or factual accuracy. The reader expects the writer to *interpret* this factual information. Consider this sentence written by Bob Shacochis in which he describes the beginning of a hurricane:

> Now, if a vortex deepened at the center of the storm and if the clouds walled up into an eye, forming a chimney for evaporating water to be sucked heavenward off the ocean—if these things happened, we'd have a hurricane: a massive, self-sustaining heat engine, siphoning excess warmth out of the ocean and taking it on a parabolic ride west and north, its intention to balance the earth's heat budget, spreading around the surplus at cooler latitudes.

Great sentence! Shacochis takes facts that are available to any writer and finds bold metaphors ("self-sustaining heat engine . . . on a parabolic ride . . . to balance the earth's heat budget") that let us see these facts in a new light.

The following essay was written by an eighth grader in New York. Like other examples of successful writing, this essay has much to commend it: voice, humor, language play. But more than anything else I am swept along by the ideas, the insight, the sheer unsentimental intelligence of this essay. After reading this essay, I can never see my relationship with my children—or parents—the same way I used to see it.

PARENTS

In all the animal kingdom, it is difficult to find a creature more proud, powerful, and predictably provocative than the Parent. Displaying a concern for their young that borders on the bothersome, members of this species have been observed exhibiting the following behaviors toward their offspring: they warn, threaten, order, judge, criticize, preach, advise, and lecture.

"Either that room gets cleaned up now, or else!"

"Can't you do anything right?"

"If I were you . . ."

"When I was your age . . ."

"You'll do as you're told."

Parents put you down, stereotype, humiliate, prophesize, nag, accuse, and name-call.

"You're acting like a baby."

"How can you be so stupid?"

"Don't you think of anyone except yourself?"

They also shame, coerce, trivialize, dash hopes, and interrogate.

"Why don't you act your age?"

"If you know what's good for you . . ."

"You're too young . . ."

They say one thing and do another. They tell you why you can't instead of how you might, what's wrong instead of what's right. It's all done in the name of love.

Some of you may think I'm being a little hard on parents. Look, I don't have anything against parents, not really. I know that there have been sightings of parents engaged in harmonious habitation with their children.

It's a funny thing in families: often, the greater the love and commitment between parents and children, the greater the conflict, the greater the hurt. It's precisely *because* people care, *because* they want to protect and guide and make over those they love in their own image, that so many problems develop. You want their love, respect, and approval, and they want yours. You have an investment in each other that you don't want to lose. It's the caring that makes you fight, and the fighting that makes you no longer care.

Now, let's get back to those bizarre birds who keep you under their wings, your parents. You remember them, the creatures with eyes in the back of their heads, and the ability to read minds. They're the ones who, out of genuine love and concern for your well-being, can do some damage. You've got to understand how they see you, how they see themselves, and how they see their role as parents.

Naturally, your parents want you to be happy, healthy, brilliant, responsible, athletic, neat, successful, honest, and well-mannered.

"Is that all?" you ask. No, not if your parents pressure you to excel. Then this modest set of expectations can only expand. All A's isn't good enough: if you're that smart, how about working harder to become valedictorian? Athletic? Well, let's see some leadership! Team captain, no less. College-bound? Could it mean anything that your mom grew ivy on the bars of your crib?

Parents can become so focused on what they want their kid to become that they lose sight of *who* their kid is. Should you be so lucky (?) to reach one of their goals, well, that's what they expect from you, your success is taken for granted and whoosh, before you can say Harvard Law School, they've swooped in with their sights on a new target.

Unfortunately, many parents judge their success as parents by the extent to which they can identify and correct "flaws" in their kids. What happens, sadly, is the destruction of the parent-child relationship. Instead of a loving, caring relationship between two *equals* (equals as human beings even if one has more experience or power than the other), you end up with a relationship based upon *roles* where the parent is dominant and the child is inferior. Once those roles are established, you can lose your identity.

It's as if you become an object instead of a person, a lump of clay that is molded. Somehow, in this Child Role you're made to feel less than equal, less than human, like a doll to be dressed and groomed in someone else's image. You lose your rights, you lose touch with your feelings, you become suspended between your parents' expectations and your true self. You become a mirror, a dream, an extension. You become property, "my kid," something to be owned. You become everything, everything except yourself.

Your parents, who seemingly have all the power, money and independence, can also feel rejected, unloved, and unappreciated. They see themselves as the people who have done more for you than anyone. They got up in the middle of the night to feed you, they sacrificed many of their plans and purchases for your benefit, and they know how important you are to their lives. This makes them feel entitled to your obedience and appreciation. When they don't get it, they feel resentful and hurt. They feel like they can't do anything right in your eyes; you've written them off as out of touch, narrow-minded, materialistic, overly concerned with what people think. You don't want to be seen with them, you don't like how they drive, what they wear, what they value.

And because of the cycle of criticism already established in the household, you lose no opportunity to peddle your disdain in their direction.

They feel ignored, misunderstood, and abused. They feel they're taken for granted, that they are seen as objects: a hander-out of money, a cooker, a cleaner, a chauffeur, a protector, a tutor. They feel stereotyped into the Parent Role, and in that role they feel that *they* are less than equal. They feel that their children don't care about them, and don't extend them courtesies that mere strangers would receive.

So just remember that they were kids just like us once. One day we'll be in *their* place.

Final Thoughts

Real writers serve their material. They allow it to pass through them and have the opportunity to move beyond the daily limitations of being inside themselves. It's like being led by a whisper.
JAYNE ANNE PHILLIPS

ONE DAY my brother Jim, a born naturalist, was exploring the woods with a bunch of fellow Boy Scouts. We spotted a small run-down shack that had caved in on one side. Jim got there first and clambered in. A moment later he emerged with a loud and exultant cry. What we saw made us gasp. He was holding two fistfuls of snakes! He had surprised them—garter snakes or grass snakes—sunning on an old piece of plywood. I will never forget the image of my brother, grinning like some modern Medusa and brandishing those snakes for everyone to see.

Isn't writing a little like that? The writer goes out into the world (or descends into the inner world) and returns with both fists clutching a mass of words, ideas, characters, places, stories, insights, possibly poisonous, hopefully not, and waves them, still squirming, still alive, before the startled reader.

Let me end this book with a few deep beliefs about writing, thoughts that didn't quite fit into the previous chapters.

Don't be afraid to live like a writer. Writers explore. There are two whole universes for you to explore—the one on the inside, and the physical one on the outside. Take your choice: inner or outer. Or best: both.

And I don't just mean exploring through words or books, though that's certainly important. I mean real exploration. "Don't let your books get in the way of your education," Mark Twain once said. In other words: live. Writers don't shy away from new experiences. If you have a chance to go somewhere new, go. Have an adventure. If you have a choice between watching a video at home or helping out at a soup kitchen for homeless people, go to the soup kitchen, out of curiosity if nothing else.

Real exploration means that you'll probably get lost. That's all right. A famous naturalist once said that you cannot really know any wilderness until you have been truly and utterly lost in that wilderness. The same could be said for the wilderness of writing.

But don't fall into the trap of thinking you must live glamorously or dangerously in some exotic locale to be a writer, either. There are poems, plays, stories, articles, novels everywhere, right under your feet, just waiting to be written. Open your eyes and the rest of your senses. Look for them where you are right now. The German poet Rainer Maria Rilke put it this way:

> If your daily life seems poor, do not blame it; blame yourself, tell yourself that you are not poet enough to call forth its riches.

Think small. The best things to write about are often the tiniest things—your brother's junk drawer, something weird your dog once did, your grandma's loose wiggly neck, changing a dirty diaper, the moment you realized you were too old to take a bath with your brother. James Michener has written a marvelous essay about writing: "Go Waste, Young Man." Michener, who did not start writing seriously until he was forty, says he has been surprised to find that the "in-between" jobs—dishwashing, work at an unemployment office—are the ones he draws on most as a writer.

Listen to people. Listen to their stories, to how they tell those stories, where they put the emphasis. Not just young people but old people, too. Old people are walking history books. These men and women have incredible stories, and most will tell them if you will listen. Young people can tell us of life's plans and hopes, but old people can tell us what life can do to those hopes.

Have courage. Who among us was born with the genius of a Stephen Hawking or the athletic genius of a Michael Jordan? Nobody I know. But I do know people with real guts, who will stand up for what they believe in. Courage is a quality available to all of us. Speak up. Let the voice in your writing be heard.

Writing is powerful stuff. The world has been altered forever by books thin as a slice of pizza. Don't be afraid to write about the wrongs and injustices of the world as you see them.

On the other hand, sometimes a writer must keep silent. James Joyce named "silence, exile, cunning" as the writer's tools. There is a part of the writer's consciousness that stands apart, observing, reflecting.

Some writing never gets shared. Certain ideas must grow very slowly inside you—you've got to give them time and room to grow. For the past few years I have had this idea for a book. I won't talk about it here—I am not ready to share it. And I can't write it. Not yet. I'm trying to grow into it. Someday I hope I can write that book. I'm trying to be patient.

There's no short cut. Writing is hard.

Read! And read some more.

Beware advice. Trust only the best ideas you find.

Live in the concrete world. Wiretap your inner voice.

Don't be afraid to put your goals high. Growing up, my favorite short story was titled "The Five-Dollar Job," about a boy who gets a job cutting a woman's lawn. The woman explains that she will pay him according to the quality of his work. An average job will earn you two dollars and fifty cents, she tells him. A good job is around three dollars, three-fifty for a very good job, a four-dollar job is just about perfect and, as for the five-dollar job, well, that's just about impossible: It's never been done so it's not worth talking about.

The boy takes the job. Week after week, he cuts her lawn. After he finishes, he surveys the yard and gives the woman an honest appraisal: "Three dollars," the first week, "Three-fifty," the next, and so on. The woman never quarrels with his price.

As the summer wears on he settles into the three dollar to three-fifty range with one or two lapses to two-fifty. But at night he dreams of the five-dollar job. It haunts him. He can't get it out of his mind. He tries picturing it, tries imagining the work necessary to complete such a feat. Every Saturday he begins with high hopes—but every time his will weakens and he falls short.

One Saturday he arrives at her house early and determined. He uses a rolling pin to smooth down all the worm holes. This nearly knocks out his energy but on that day he discovers a secret: the catnap. He lies down and takes a nap under a big tree. When he wakes up ten minutes later he feels totally refreshed. Back to work. He cuts the lawn twice, first one way, then another, the way they do it at major league baseball stadiums. He adds about a dozen other extra touches (interspersed with several more catnaps) until that lawn fairly sparkles. Twilight has begun to fall when he knocks on the woman's door.

"How much this week?" she asks him.

"Five dollars, ma'am," he replies without hesitation.

"I thought I said the five-dollar job was impossible."

"I know you did," he answers her. "But I just did it."

She pauses and looks at him closely.

"Well, if this is the first five-dollar job in history, I guess it's worth taking a look at," she says.

They walked the lawn together. Even he is amazed at how stunningly beautiful it looks. The woman turns to look at him.

"Young man, you did something great today," she says.

Writing a book about writing has left me with an intense thirst to write about something else. As I reach the end I can feel all sorts of poems, stories, and novels tugging at my mind's sleeve. If this book inspires anyone else to write, well then, I will consider it a job well done.

Appendix

Someone once quipped that the purpose of a list is to start an argument. Why is that book *on the list? Why did you exclude* this?

What follows is not meant to be "the list" but rather some of the books, poems, and stories my students and I have found useful in thinking about character, setting, time, voice, etc. I would be grateful to receive suggestions for texts to add to these lists.

BOOKS ABOUT WORDS AND WORD-PLAY

Webster's New Universal Unabridged Dictionary.
Mrs. Byrne's Dictionary of Unusual, Obscure, and Preposterous Words, by Josefa H. Byrne (Citadel).
Words, by Paul Dickson (Delacorte Press).
Books by Richard Lederer, including *The Miracle of Language* and *The Play of Words: Fun and Games For Language Lovers* (Whitney). Also, *Get Thee to a Punnery* (Dell).
Wordstruck, by Robert McNeil (Viking Penguin).
Morris Dictionary of Words and Phrase Origins, by William and Mary Morris (HarperCollins).

For Young Writers and Readers

A Book of Puzzlements: Play and Invention with Language, by Herbert Kohl (Schocken Books, Pantheon, Random House).
The King Who Rained and *A Little Pigeon Toad,* by Fred Gwynne (Simon & Schuster). Funny and engaging books about common expressions of speech.
Merry Go Round (A Book About Nouns) and *Kites Sail High (A Book About Verbs),* by Ruth Heller (Grosset & Dunlap). These books encourage young writers to start thinking about words. Also, *Many Luscious Lolli-pops (A Book About Adjectives)* and *A Cache of Jewels (And Other Collective Nouns).*
A First Thesaurus, by Harriet Wittels and Joan Greisman (Golden/Western).

MEMOIRS

The following books give insight into the mentors and early experiences that formed a writer's sensibility. I am indebted to Suzanne Gardinier for providing many of the titles on this list.

A Grain of Wheat, by Clyde Robert Bulla (Godine).

A Girl from Yamhill, by Beverly Cleary (Dell).

Boy, by Roald Dahl (Penguin).

Homesick: My Own Story, by Jean Fritz (Putnam). Also *China Homecoming*.

Speaking for Ourselves, autobiographical sketches by notable authors of books for young adults, compiled by Donald R. Gallo (NCTE).

Child Times: A Three Generation Memoir, by Eloise Greenfield and Lessie Jones Little (Crowell).

Self Portrait: Trina Schart Hyman, (Harper & Row).

Little By Little, Jean Little (Viking).

Starting from Home: A Writer's Beginnings, by Milton Meltzer (Viking).

How I Came to Be a Writer, by Phyllis R. Naylor (Aladdin/Macmillan).

Bill Peet: An Autobiography (Houghton Mifflin).

But I'll Be Back Again: An Album, by Cynthia Rylant (Orchard).

My Diary—My World, By Elizabeth Yates (Westminster).

For Older Readers

I Know Why the Caged Bird Sings, by Maya Angelou (Random House).

Growing Up, by Russell Baker (Signet).

No Name in the Street and *Go Tell It on the Mountain*, by James Baldwin (Dell).

Stop-Time, by Frank Conroy (Viking).

An American Childhood, by Annie Dillard (Harper & Row).

The Open Door: When Writers First Learned To Read, by Steven Gilbar (David R. Godine).

Strive for Freedom, by Martin Luther King, Jr. (Harper & Row).

Kaffir Boy, by Mark Mathabane (Plume).

Black Boy, by Richard Wright (Harper & Row).

One Writer's Beginnings, by Eudora Welty (Warner Books).

Inventing the Truth, The Art and Craft of Memoir, edited by William Zinsser (Houghton Mifflin).

SOME NOTABLE BEGINNINGS

1. One day last spring, Louis, a butcher, turned into a fish. Silvery scales. Big lips. A tail. A salmon.

Louis the Fish, by Arthur Yorinks

2. And how's my little girl?
Granpa, by John Burningham

3. It was in the summer of the year when the relatives came. They came up from Virginia. They left when their grapes were nearly purple enough to pick, but not quite.
The Relatives Came, by Cynthia Rylant

4. On a summer evening
    I looked up from dinner,
    through the open window to the backyard.
    Fireflies!, by Julie Brinckloe

5. Here is James Henry Trotter when he was about four years old.
    Up until this time, he had had a happy life, living peacefully with his mother and father in a beautiful house beside the sea. There were always plenty of other children for him to play with, and there was the sandy beach for him to run about on, and the ocean to paddle in. It was the perfect life for a small boy.
    Then, one day, James' mother and father went to London to do some shopping, and there a terrible thing happened. Both of them suddenly got eaten up (in full daylight, mind you, and on a crowded street) by an enormous angry rhinoceros which had escaped from the London Zoo.
    James and the Giant Peach, by Roald Dahl

6. If you are a child who is never told the truth, you begin to make up your own. After my father left, and no one mentioned his name again, I simply made up things about him.
But I'll Be Back Again, by Cynthia Rylant

7. Once upon a time there was a bat—a little light brown bat, the color of coffee with cream in it. He looked like a furry mouse with wings.
The Bat Poet, by Randall Jarrell

8. The Iron Man came to the top of the cliff.
    How far had he walked? Nobody knows. Where had he come from? Nobody knows. How was he made? Nobody knows.
    The Iron Man, by Ted Hughes

9. His mother was ugly and his father was ugly, but Shreck was uglier than the two of them put together.
Shreck!, by William Steig

10. I will always remember when the stars fell down around me and lifted me up above the George Washington Bridge.
Tar Beach, by Faith Ringgold

ENDINGS

Surprise Endings

Picture Books

Just Like Daddy, by Frank Asch (for young children) (Prentice-Hall).
The Wednesday Surprise, by Eve Bunting (Clarion).

Just Like Everyone Else, by Karla Kuskin (Harper Trophy).

Flossie and the Fox, by Patricia C. McKissack (Dial).

In the Attic, by Hiawyn Oram (Henry Holt).

Super Dooper Jezebel, by Tony Ross (Farrar, Straus).

The Frog Prince, by Jon Scieszka (Viking).

Earthlets, by Jeanne Willis (Dutton).

Novels and Short Stories

"The Two Brothers," by Lloyd Alexander, in *The Big Book for Peace* (Dutton).

Roald Dahl's short stories for adults: "Royal Jelly," among others; from *The Roald Dahl Omnibus* (Dorset).

The Gift of the Magi, by O. Henry (Bantam). Many of O. Henry's short stories have surprise endings.

Circular Endings

Picture Books

Very Last First Time, by Jan Andrews (Groundwood, Vancouver).

Grandfather Twilight, by Barbara Berger (Philomel).

"Poem," by Langston Hughes, in *Best Friends*, edited by Lee Bennet Hopkins (Harper & Row).

If You Give a Mouse a Cookie, by Laura J. Numeroff (Scholastic). Also, *If You Give a Moose a Muffin*.

A Winter Place, by Ruth Yaffe Radin (Atlantic, Reading Rainbow).

The Relatives Came, by Cynthia Rylant (Bradbury Press). Also *Birthday Presents*.

Two Bad Ants, by Chris Van Allsburg (Houghton Mifflin).

Louis the Fish, by Arthur Yorinks (Farrar, Straus).

Bob and Shirley, by Harriet Ziefert (HarperCollins).

Novels

Flowers for Algernon, by Daniel Keyes (Bantam).

A Wrinkle in Time, by Madeleine L'Engle

The Journey, by Patricia MacLachlan (Harper & Row).

The Hobbit, by J. R. Tolkien.

Poignant Endings

Picture Books

The Children We Remember, by Chana Byers Abells (Greenwillow). This very powerful book deals with the Holocaust.

The Two of Them, by Aliki (Greenwillow).

Gorilla, by Anthony Browne (Knopf).

Dear Daddy, by Phillipe Dupasquier (Bradbury Press).

Wilfred Gordon McDonald Partridge, by Mem Fox (Kane/Miller).

The Ring and the Window Seat, by Amy Hest (Scholastic).

The Year of the Perfect Christmas Tree, by Barbara Houston (Dial).

The Keeping Quilt, by Patricia Polacco (Simon & Schuster).

Faithful Elephants, by Yukio Tsuchiya (Houghton Mifflin).

A Father Like That, by Charlotte Zolotow (Harper & Row). Also *William's Doll.*

Novels and Short Stories

On My Honor, by M. D. Bauer (Dell).

Sadako and the Thousand Paper Cranes, by Eleanor Coerr (Dell).

8 Plus 1 Stories, by Robert Cormier (Bantam).

Hare's Choice, by Dennis Hamley (Delacorte).

Throwing Shadows, short stories by E. L. Konigsburg (Macmillan).

Bridge to Terabithia, by Katherine Paterson (Harper & Row).

"Slower than the Rest," short story in *Every Living Thing,* by Cynthia Rylant (Aladdin).

Ambiguous Endings

"A Worn Path," short story by Eudora Welty.

Where the Forest Meets the Sea, by Jeannie Baker (Greenwillow).

Granpa, by John Burningham (Crown).

BOOKS WITH STRONG CHARACTERS

Picture Books

The Two of Them, by Aliki (Greenwillow).

The Song and Dance Man, by Karen Ackerman (Knopf).

Granpa, by John Burningham (Crown).

My Mother's House, My Father's House, by C. B. Christiansen (Atheneum).

Molly's Pilgrim, Barbara Cohen (Lothrop).

Miss Rumphius, by Barbara Cooney (Viking).

An Enchanted Hair Tale, by Alexis De Veaux (Harper and Row).

Diana, Maybe, by Crescent Dragonwagon (Macmillan).

How Does It Feel to Be Old? by Norma Farber (Creative Arts Book Co., 833 Bancroft Way, Berkeley, CA 9410).

Rosalie, by Jean Hewett (Lothrop).

Tales of a Gambling Grandma, by Dayal Kaur Khalsa (Potter/Crown).

Through Grandpa's Eyes, by Patricia MacLachlan (Harper & Row).

Super Dooper Jezebel, by Tony Ross (Farrar, Straus).

Mr. Grigg's Work, by Cynthia Rylant (Orchard).
Many books by William Steig, including *Amos and Boris*.
Crow Boy, by Taro Yashima (Viking).
Books by Arthur Yorinks, including *Hey, Al* and *Louis the Fish* (Farrar, Straus).
I Know a Lady, by Charlotte Zolotow (Picture Puffin); also *William's Doll*.

Novels

Go Ask Alice, anonymous, (Avon).
Tuck Everlasting, by Natalie Babbitt (Farrar, Straus).
Home Before Dark, by Sue Ellen Bridgers (Bantam).
The Stories Julian Tells and *More Stories Julian Tells*, by Ann Cameron (Pantheon).
The Ramona books by Beverly Cleary.
"The Mustache," in *8 Plus 1 Stories*, by Robert Cormier (Bantam).
Charlie and the Chocolate Factory and *Matilda*, by Roald Dahl (Puffin Penguin).
The Outsiders, by S. E. Hinton (Dell).
Bunnicula, by Deborah and James Howe (Avon).
Books by Jack London, especially *White Fang* and *The Call of the Wild*.
Hey World Here I Am, by Jean Little (Harper Trophy).
Autumn Street, by Lois Lowry (Dell).
Goodnight, Mr. Tom, by Michelle Margorian (Harper & Row).
Member of the Wedding, by Carson McCullers (Bantam).
Anything by Katherine Paterson, especially *The Great Gilly Hopkins* and *Bridge to Terabithia* (Harper & Row).
Maniac Magee, by Jerry Spinelli (Little, Brown).
Dicey's Song and *Homecoming*, by Cynthia Voigt (Fawcett).

Novels for Older Readers

Cold Sassy Tree, by Olive Ann Burns.
Mrs. Bridge and *Mr. Bridge*, by Evan S. Connell (North Point Press).
Yellow Raft in Blue Water, by Michael Dorris (Warner).
Ironweed, by William Kennedy (Viking).
One Flew Over the Cuckoo's Nest and *Sometimes A Great Notion*, by Ken Kesey.
Love in the Time of Cholera, by Gabriel Garcia Márquez (Harper & Row).
Anywhere But Here, by Mona Simpson (Knopf).
The Joy Luck Club, by Any Tan (Knopf).
Anything by Tolstoy.
Novels of Anne Tyler.

VOICE

Picture Books

The Pain and the Great One, by Judy Blume (Dell).
Goodbye Geese, by Nancy Carlstrom (Philomel).
An Enchanted Hair Tale, by Alexis De Veaux (Harper & Row).
On the Day You Were Born, by Debra Frasier (HBJ).
Tight Times, by Barbara Shook Hazen (Puffin).
Anniranni and Mollymishi, by C. Drew Lamm (Annick Press, Toronto).
I Am the Ocean, by Suzanna Marshak (Arcade).
Books by Bill Martin, Jr. and John Archambault, especially *White Dynamite and the Curly Kid* and *Knots on a Counting Rope* (Henry Holt).
The Keeping Quilt, by Patricia Polacco (Simon & Schuster).
Books by Cynthia Rylant, especially *The Relatives Came* (Bradbury Press), *The Soda Jerk,* poetry (Orchard), and *When I Was Young in the Mountains* (Dutton).
The Three Little Pigs, by John Scieszka (Viking).
Gila Monsters Meet You at the Airport, by Marjorie Sharmat (Macmillan).
Stevie and *My Special Best Words,* by John Steptoe (Harper & Row).

Short Stories and Novels

Black Elk Speaks (University of Nebraska Press).
The Education of Little Tree, by Forrest Carter (University of New Mexico Press).
Anything by Roald Dahl, for example, *Boy* (Puffin).
Love Medicine, by Louise Erdrich (Bantam).
All I Really Wanted to Know I Learned in Kindergarten, pages 13–16, by Robert Fulghum (Ivy Book).
That Was Then, This Is Now, by S. E. Hinton (Dell).
Little Little, by M. E. Kerr (Bantam).
Flowers for Algernon, by Daniel Keyes (Bantam).
Autumn Street, by Lois Lowry (Dell).
So Much to Tell You, by John Marsden (Fawcett).
But I'll Be Back Again, by Cynthia Rylant (Orchard).
The Catcher in the Rye, by J. D. Salinger (Little, Brown).
A Taste of Blackberries, by Doris B. Smith (Crowell).
Night, by Elie Wiesel (Bantam).

Nonfiction

A Medieval Feast by Aliki (Harper Trophy).
Where the Forest Meets the Sea by Jeannie Baker (Greenwillow).

Books by Byrd Baylor including *The Way To Start The Day* (Aladdin Books).

A River Ran Wild and *The Great Kapok Tree* by Lynne Cherry (Gulliver, HBJ).

The Magic School Bus series by Joanna Cole (Scholastic).

The Popcorn Book by Tomie de Paola (Holiday House).

Arctic Memories by Normee Ekoomiak (Henry Holt).

Time Train by Paul Fleishman (HarperCollins).

Books by Jean Fritz about the American Revolution (Coward-McCann).

All Upon A Sidewalk by Jean Craighead George (Dutton).

Box Turtle by William T. George (Greenwillow).

A Little Schubert by M.B. Goffstein (Godine).

Ox-Cart Man by Donald Hall (Picture Puffin).

The Comet And You by E.C. Krupp (Macmillan).

A Prarie Boy's Winter by William Kurelek (Houghton-Mifflin).

The Microscope by Maxine Kumin (Harper Trophy, Reading Rainbow).

The Philharmonica Gets Dressed and *The Dallas Titans Get Ready For Bed* by Karla Kuskin (Harper and Row).

Hiroshima No Pika by Maruki (Lothrop, Lee and Shepard). The destruction of Hiroshima by the atomic bomb.

BUGS by Nancy Winslow Parker and Joan Richards Wright. (Mulberry Books).

Chipmunk Song by Joanne Ryder (Lodestar/Dutton). Also *The Snail's Spell*.

How Much Is A Million? by David M. Schwartz (Scholastic).

Nettie's Trip South by Ann Turner (Macmillan).

For Younger Readers

A Snake Is Totally Tail by Judi Barrett (Aladdin Books).

Books by Eric Carle including *The Very Busy Spider* and *The Very Hungry Caterpillar* (Picture Books Studio).

In My Garden, In The Woods, The Spider In Its Web, by Ermanno Cristini and Luigi Puricelli (Picture Book Studio).

A House Is A House For Me by Mary Ann Hoberman (Puffin Books).

The Carrot Seed by Ruth Krauss (Harper and Row).

Farm Alphabet by Jane Miller (Scholastic).

Egg to Chick by Millicent E. Selsam (Harper Trophy).

Early Morning In The Barn by Nancy Tafuri (Picture Puffin).

BOOKS WITH A DISTINCT SENSE OF PLACE

Picture Books

Very Last First Time, by Jan Andrews (Groundwood, Toronto).

Where the Forest Meets the Sea, by Jeannie Baker (Greenwillow).

Many books by Byrd Baylor, including *Your Own Secret Place, The Desert Is Theirs* and *The Best Town in the World* (Scribners).

The Tunnel, by Anthony Browne (Knopf).

The Great Kapok Tree, by Lynne Cherry (Harcourt Brace).

Miss Rumphius, by Barbara Cooney (Viking).

Arctic Memories, by Normee Ekoomiak (Henry Holt).

Snow White in New York, by Fiona French (Oxford).

Box Turtle at Long Pond, by William T. George (Greenwillow).

Up North in Winter, by Deborah Hartley (Dutton).

In Coal Country, by Judith Hendershot (Knopf).

The Year of the Perfect Christmas Tree, by Gloria Houston (Dial).

Yonder, by Tony Johnston (Dial).

Night Ride, by Bernie and Mati Karlin (Simon & Schuster).

The Beach Before Breakfast, by Maxine W. Kumin (Putnam).

My Little Island, by Frane Lessac (Lippincott).

Where the River Begins, by Thomas Locker (Dial).

I Am the Ocean, by Suzanna Marshak (Arcade).

In the Attic, by Hiawyn Oram (Henry Holt).

Woodpile, by Peter Parnall (Macmillan).

The Chalk Doll, by Charlotte Pomerantz (Lippincott).

Once There Was a Tree, by N. Romanova (Dial).

Inside Turtle's Shell, by Joanne Ryder (Macmillan). Poetry.

All I See, by Cynthia Rylant (Orchard Books); also *When I Was Young in the Mountains* (Dutton), *Appalachia,* and *Night in the Country* (Bradbury Press).

Sierra, by Diane Siebert (HarperCollins).

No Star Nights, by Anna Egan Smucker (Knopf).

Mufaro's Beautiful Daughters, by John Steptoe (Lothrop).

Dakota Dugout, by Ann Turner (Macmillan).

Three Days on a River in a Red Canoe, by Vera B. Williams (Mulberry).

Owl Moon, by Jane Yolen (Philomel).

Novels

Tuck Everlasting, by Natalie Babbitt (Farrar, Straus).

Prairie Songs, by Pam Conrad (Trumpet).

From the Mixed-up Files of Mrs. Basil E. Frankweiler, by E. L. Konigsburg (Dell).

Anything by Jean Craighead George, especially *Julie of the Wolves* (Harper & Row).

The Contender, by Robert Lipsyte (Bantam).

Anything by Jack London.

Sarah, Plain and Tall, by Patricia MacLachlan (HarperCollins).

Anything by Gary Paulsen.

TIME

These books contain a vivid or unusual use of time.

Picture Books

The Two of Them, by Aliki (Greenwillow).

Granpa, by John Burningham (Crown). Written snapshots of individual moments between a grandfather and granddaughter.

I'm in Charge of Celebrations, by Byrd Baylor (Scribners).

In Coal Country, by Judith Hendershot (Knopf).

Rosalie, by Joan Hewett (Lothrop).

When I Was Young in the Mountains, by Cynthia Rylant (Dutton).

When I Was Nine, by James Stevenson (Greenwillow).

Everett Anderson's Goodbye, by Lucille Clifton (Holt); also *Some of the Days of Everett Anderson.*

Home Place, by Crescent Dragonwagon (Macmillan).

Time Train, by Paul Fleischman (HarperCollins).

Julie of the Wolves, by Jean Craighead George (Harper & Row). Flashback.

Ring and the Window Seat, by Amy Hest (Scholastic).

The Beach Before Breakfast, by Maxine W. Kumin (Putnam).

The Stopwatch, by David Lloyd (Harper & Row).

Karin's Christmas Walk, by Susan Pearson (Dial).

Night in the Country, by Cynthia Rylant (Bradbury).

Stevie, by John Steptoe (Harper & Row).

Just a Dream, by Chris Van Allsburg (Houghton Mifflin).

A Chair for My Mother, by Vera B. Williams (Mulberry). Flashback.

Novels

Autumn Street, by Lois Lowry (Dell).

Sarah, Plain and Tall, by Patricia MacLachlan (Harper & Row). Flashback.

Dogsong, by Gary Paulsen (Puffin Books). Real time and dream time woven together; also *Hatchet.*

TENSION/CONFLICT

Person versus Person

Picture Books

Old Henry, by Joan W. Blos (Morrow).

Piggybook, by Anthony Browne (Knopf).

Hiroshima No Pika, by Toshi Maruki (Lothrop).

The Big Orange Splot, by Daniel Pinkwater (Scholastic).
Lizard's Song, by George Shannon (Greenwillow).
Crowboy, by Taro Yashima (Viking).

Novels and Short Stories
Summer of the Swans, by Betsy Byars (Puffin).
Woman Who Flummoxed the Fairies, by Heather Forrest (HBJ).
Call of the Wild, by Jack London.
Kaffir Boy, by Mark Mathabane (Plume).
Number the Stars, by Lois Lowry (Dell).
War with Grandpa, by Robert K. Smith (Dell).
Naya Nuki—Girl Who Ran, by K. Thomasma (Voyager).
"The Most Dangerous Game," short story by Richard Connell.

Person versus Nature

Picture Books
Where the Forest Meets the Sea and *Window,* by Jeannie Baker (Greenwillow).
The Great Kapok Tree, by Lynne Cherry (Harcourt Brace).
We're Going on a Bear Hunt, by Michael Rosen (McElderry).
Brave Irene and *Amos and Boris,* by William Steig (Farrar, Straus).
Just a Dream, by Chris Van Allsburg (Houghton Mifflin).

Novels and Short Stories
Prairie Songs by Pam Conrad (HarperCollins).
Julie of the Wolves, by Jean Craighead George (Harper & Row); also *My Side of the Mountain* and *The Other Side of the Mountain.*
Never Cry Wolf, by Farley Mowat (Bantam).
Island of the Blue Dolphins, by Scott O'Dell (Dell).
Dogsong, Hatchet, and *Woodsong* by Gary Paulsen.
"To Build a Fire," short story by Jack London, in *The Collected Jack London,* edited by Steven J. Kasdin (Dorset).

Inner Conflict

Picture Books
Fang (Atheneum) and *My Mom Travels a Lot,* by Caroline Feller Bauer (Frederick Warne). For younger children.
Everett Anderson's Nine Month Long, by Lucille Clifton (Henry Holt).
Annie and the Old One, by Miska Miles (Little, Brown).
Miss Maggie, by Cynthia Rylant (Dutton).
Gila Monsters Meet You at the Airport, by Marjorie Sharmat (Macmillan); also *I Want Mama* for young children.

Faithful Elephants, by Yukio Tsuchiya (Houghton Mifflin).

Nettie's Trip South, by Ann Turner (Macmillan).

A Tiger for Thomas, by Charlotte Zolotow (Harper & Row).

Novels and Short Stories

The One-Eyed Cat, by Paula Fox (Dell).

Beast and the Halloween Horror, by Patricia Reilly Giff (Dell); also *Candy Corn Contest*.

A Solitary Blue, by Cynthia Voigt (Fawcett).

Ira Sleeps Over, by Bernard Waber (Houghton Mifflin); also *Ira Says Goodbye*.

The Castle in the Attic, by E. Winthrop (Scholastic).

BOOKS WITH UNFORGETTABLE LANGUAGE

Picture Books

Stina, by Lena Anderson (Greenwillow).

Very Last First Time, by Jan Andrews (Groundwood). This picture book is published in Toronto—it is a treasure!

Books by Byrd Baylor, especially *I'm in Charge of Celebrations* (Scribners) and *Guess Who My Favorite Person Is* (Atheneum). Nearly all Baylor's books have a distinctive poetic quality.

Fireflies, by Julie Brinckloe (Aladdin paperback).

Goodbye Geese, by Nancy White Carlstrom (Philomel).

The Great Kapok Tree, by Lynne Cherry ((Harcourt Brace).

When Light Turns Into Dark, by Crescent Dragonwagon (Harper & Row).

When You Were Born, by Debra Frasier (Harcourt Brace).

A House Is a House for Me, by Mary Ann Hoberman (Viking).

Anniranni and Mollymishi, by C. Drew Lamm (Annick Press, Toronto).

I Am the Ocean, by Suzanna Marshak (Little, Brown).

Anything by Bill Martin, Jr., especially *The Ghost-Eye Tree* and *Listen to the Rain* (Henry Holt).

Grandpa Loved, by Josephine Nobisso (Green Tiger Press).

Woodpile, by Peter Parnall (Macmillan).

Tar Beach, by Faith Ringgold (Crown).

Sierra and *Mohave*, by Diane Siebert (HarperCollins).

Books by William Steig, especially *Brave Irene* and *Amos and Boris* (Farrar, Straus).

My Special Best Words, by John Steptoe (Viking).

More More More Said the Baby, by Vera B. Williams (Greenwillow).

Owl Moon, by Jane Yolen (Philomel).

Poetry

Jabberwocky, by Lewis Carroll (Frederick Warne).

Hist Wist, by e.e. cummings (Crown).

Joyful Noise, Poems for Two Voices, by Paul Fleischman (Harper & Row); also *Rondo in C.*

Honey, I Love, and other poems by Eloise Greenfield (Crowell).

"From Mother To Son," poem by Langston Hughes.

Pocket Poems and *The Place My Words Are Looking For,* poetry anthologies edited by Paul B. Janeczko (Bradbury Press).

Secrets of a Small Brother, poems by Richard Margolis (Macmillan).

The Soda Jerk, by Cynthia Rylant (Orchard Books).

Almost anything by William Carlos Williams.

Many Winters, by Nancy Wood (Doubleday).

All the Small Poems, by Valerie Worth (Farrar, Straus).

Novels

Tuck Everlasting, by Natalie Babbit (Farrar Straus). A novel with some remarkable descriptive passages.

Taking the Ferry Home, by Pam Conrad (Harper & Row).

I Heard the Owl Call My Name, by Margaret Craven (Totem).

The BFG, by Roald Dahl (Penguin).

Borning Room, by Paul Fleischman (HarperCollins).

"Clothes" and "Oranges," in *Hey World Here I Am,* by Jean Little (Harper & Row).

Ceremony, by Leslie M. Silko.

Other Novels

A Death in the Family, by James Agee (Bantam).

Money, by Martin Amis (Penguin).

Novels by Saul Bellow.

An American Childhood, by Annie Dillard (Harper & Row).

Love Medicine, by Louise Erdrich (Bantam).

Ironweed, by William Kennedy (Penguin).

The Book of Laughter and Forgetting, by Milan Kundera (Penguin).

Novels by Toni Morrison, especially *Beloved* (Knopf).

Woman Hollering Creek, Sandra Cisneros (Vintage).

Housekeeping, Mariylnne Robinson (Bantam).

Index

INDEX